CREDIT SCORE

The System of Clear Credit Shows You How to Legally Repair Your Credit

(Great Credit Repair Tips to Increase Your Credit Score)

David Brown

Published by Knowledge Icons

David Brown

All Rights Reserved

Credit Score: The System of Clear Credit Shows You How to Legally Repair Your Credit (Great Credit Repair Tips to Increase Your Credit Score)

ISBN 978-1-990084-71-3

Legal & Disclaimer

TABLE OF CONTENTS

Introduction

Every time you take out your credit card and put it to use, your purchase, as well as how and when you pay it off, will contribute to your credit score. The credit score is not just another number that you can afford to not take seriously. Too many people fail to realize that in the future, when they want to purchase big ticket items such as houses, their credit score will have a major say whether this goes ahead or stalls.

A low credit score, among other things, will block you from being able to purchase your desired item or make things a lot more difficult for you by compelling the financial institution you approach to attach higher-than-average interest rates, or insist that you clear up your credit in a shorter period. Surely, this is in no way an ideal situation, or is it?

A high credit score, on the other hand, makes things a lot easier. Buying a house, for instance, becomes less complicated. You will be able to buy your item smoothly without having absurd interest rates attached, or have to pay off your credit amount in a short time window. Simply put, a healthy credit score will make your financial life easier.

If your credit score is nothing close to being good, you can agree with me that accessing credit and other financial services is never easy. Banks, insurance companies and even some employers these days check your credit score to determine how much to charge for various products and for various other purposes. This essentially means that having your credit score as high as possible should be top on your priority list, especially if you have any hopes of accessing credit or using various other financial services.

This book is there for you; it will help you to understand how to improve your credit by having different items that may be hurting your score removed. Let's begin.

Thanks again for downloading this book. I hope you enjoy it!

Chapter 1: A Brief History Of The Credit

Card And The Rise Of The Fico Score

To put it most simply, a credit score determines the likelihood that you will pay your bill on time and with consistency. If someone were to ask you what the likelihood is that you'd pay a loan back on time and with recurring payments, your answer to the question might be a bit winded and lengthy. The simplicity of a credit score eliminates the need for banks to write down long summaries about a borrower's credit history. Instead of recording each and every nuance of a person's life, the credit score rises forty points or decreases by one hundred points depending on the validity of your payments. You can look at your credit score as being a reflection of your life circumstances at a given time. For example, say that someone close to you got sick and you were responsible for paying their medical bills. Paying hospital bills limited your ability to pay your credit card bills for a few months. Instead of explaining this to the bank, your bank simply recognizes that you missed some payments and penalizes your credit score to serve as a reflection of your payment inactivity. In this way, your credit score can be interpreted as an indication of how your life is operating and how responsibly you act towards paying back the banks that have lent you money. This chapter will primarily focus on why your credit score matters today, and how credit cards came to be a major factor in global transactions.

Really Quick: A Brief History of the Credit Card

The credit card itself was invented in 1950; however, the notion of using credit as way to exchange goods and services has been around since the 1800s. The first companies to offer and issues credit cards were mostly department stores and oil companies, who had a lot of consistent customers who were frequent buyers.

During its onset, these cards were only eligible at the stores that were offering them. The primary goals of these cards were to increase customer loyalty as well as customer satisfaction. The idea was that people were likely to purchase more at the stores in which they owned credit cards if they felt that they were being trusted to pay back the stores within a timely manner. Because the internet did not yet exist and there were less stores in business, customer loyalty was generally easier to maintain than it is today.

While the department store and oil company credit cards are usually known for being more popular in modern history (especially throughout Victorian British history), the first credit card that was issued by a bank originated a few years prior, in 1946. Initially, the credit card process was fairly simple; only the bank, the merchant, and the consumer were involved in the transaction. Overtime, this process has grown in present day to include that banks who want to involve themselves with credit card procedures must first join an association that works within a broader network of various banks throughout the country. Currently, MasterCard and Visa own competing credit card associations, and members must choose which company they'd like to work with before joining. This consolidation of banks into two associations broadly gives the banks who are lending their funds to credit card holders much more security than was possible when the credit card first emerged into the global marketplace. Of course, there are many more details that can be researched about the history of the credit card, but this is simply a broad overview that will hopefully better acquaint you with a brief historical account of how credit conglomerations thrive in the present day.

Of course, even back then interest was charged to money that was borrowed by the bank's consumers. The problem that the banks were finding was that they had no definitive way to determine whether or not someone was going to make their credit card payments on time. There was no history on anyone, so it was as if the banks were meeting these consumers for the first time and blindly agreeing to front an individual money. For example, in the early days of credit cards, a banking representative would contact the merchant whose customer was using one of their credit cards and inquire as to whether or not the consumer was making payments on time. Additionally, the idea of "character-based" credit was a real phenomenon and its implications are immediate reasons why an autonomous credit worthiness solution was needed. There are many early accounts of people going into a bank and asking for a loan. In these early instances, it wouldn't be uncommon for the banker to deny the individual a loan simply based on the individual's demeanor. Overtime, a legitimate scoring system was worked out by banks in order to determine who was worthy to receive a loan, but the system was clunky and still widely dependent upon emotional, rather than logical judgement. The banks needed more security in order to ensure that a profit was inevitable. This idea becomes more tangible if you think of it as the banks needing proof that the person borrowing money was reliable, just as you or I would if we were to consider lending money to a friend or loved one. There was a void the needed filling, and a company named FICO fulfilled the bank's temporary void.

The Rise of FICO

FICO stands for Fair, Isaac and Company and originated as a data analytics company in 1956, just six years after the first credit cards were passed to consumers in the United States. This company, beyond simply helping the banks to better trust the borrowing ability of their customers, revolutionized the way in which banks perceived their borrowers by creating algorithms that can indicate how reliable a borrower is. The credit score numbering system ranges between 300 to 850. Today, FICO develops other software to help businesses manage risk and helps to fight against financial fraud. Other areas in which FICO works include computer cloud memory storage technology and serves to help individual consumers maintain and grow their credit history. FICO is a major player on the New York Stock Exchange. Currently, a share of FICO stock costs $127.39. It's safe to say that FICO, since it's implementation of the credit score algorithms, have become a powerhouse within the stock market and continue will continue to be key player in both the national and international economy for years into the future.

Now that you know how the notion of the credit score came to be, you might still be asking yourself why is a credit score so important? Of course, we have broadly stated in the introduction that a credit score is what makes you reliable in the eyes of the banks, but knowing exactly how your credit score can impact your life should be explained. Knowing why your credit score matters is the first step in understanding how your actions as a consumer influence how you're financially perceived. You may know this already, but it's worth restating as a refresher. Here is a breakdown of the five factors that affect your credit:

35% is a reflection of your payment history. This not only looks at whether or not you paid your bills on time, but also how late your payments were if you paid late. The later the payment, the more negative the credit score.

30% is an analysis of how much money you owe in total. The credit score assesses how much you owe across all of your credit cards, in sum. For this section, it's good to have different types of credit, so that you can prove that you manage many types of money responsibly.

15% is based on how long you have been using credit to pay for goods. This is why it's advisable to open credit accounts when you're young. Even if you haven't opened an account until recently, showing that you are making payments on time and with consistency is more important than having a long credit history.

10% accounts for how many new lines of credit you open and how frequently. The assumption is that the more lines of credit you take out at once, the more cash flow problems you are having during a given period. If you open multiple lines of credit within the same time frame, you are considered a higher risk than if you limit the amount of accounts you have.

10% of your credit score is a reflection of the different types of credit you are currently using. The types of borrowing that the credit score looks for include credit cards, store credit card accounts, loans where the total amount is paid in installments, and mortgage loans. If you don't have all of these types of credit accounted for, the general rule is to not worry about it. This aspect of the credit score is small and only accounts for a small percentage of your overall score.

Now that you understand broadly how a credit score is generated and the history surrounding how the credit score came to be, you should be able to better understand both the capacities of credit and its limitations. While a credit score can be interpreted as a consolidated reflection of your spending tendencies, you should be able to decipher how you want to go about establishing or altering how you apply for credit. It's important to remember that FICO is king in terms of how your credit is perceived. You have to work within their guidelines if you ever want to establish a good credit score for yourself. Knowing the history of credit can also serve to help you understand how trust and credit interact. It's important that your creditors trust you so that they will continue to help you financially.

Chapter 2: Credit & Credit Reports

What is Credit?

As a concrete and simple example, if you borrow money from your friend or you asked for her to babysit and then you promised to pay her at a later time or at a certain date; or if you do not have the money now to pay for a good or service that you need, but you promise the person you are buying from that you will pay him or her on a certain date, then that is a credit. It is basically borrowing the goods or service for now and then returning it later monetarily. Many years ago, merchants would allow their customers or mainly the people they know well, to shop for their groceries and pay for it at a certain date –their pay day for example – and they would book the information in their own credit accounts. If this customer is able to make the payment on or before the promised date, then the merchant might let the customer get more items from the store, as the merchant is already certain that this customer will pay. However, if you are unable to pay on time or you never settled it, you might not be allowed to place a credit on the goods anymore. The merchant might take that information to warn the other merchants about that incident involving your credit, and it might affect how they would allow you to place a credit with them.

Today, stores have become bigger, and are now owned by big and high-end companies and corporations who allow payments via cash, check or credit card only. As years go on, more and more businessmen would be more cautious in lending money, good or services to people just so they won't lose. Because of this, certain security measures like background checks and credit scores are put into place. This is to ensure that the consumers can pay for what they owed.

A Brief History Of Credit Reporting

More than a hundred years ago, back when supermarkets are just small stalls manned by a family member who owns the small business, lending in any kind has already been a practice. And, just like any humble beginnings, these small retail merchants befriended other merchants and discussed among themselves their customer's profile, and then started trading customer's financial information with other business owners through a formed merchant's organization. As years go on, these organizations would grow larger as more businesses join in, and more and more organizations will form. The information that was once written by hand became typewritten, filed in folders, until the age of computers rise and all information became digital.

Retail Credit Company, predecessor of Equifax, was the first to start in collecting and selling consumer information to businesses and organizations. It was founded by Atlanta businessman Cator Woolford in 1899, and was the first ever Credit Reporting Agency (CRA). The industry of CRA then started to grow slowly, and then gave birth to TransUnion in the late 60's.

However, a controversy broke in the 1960's about the credit reports given by these companies. From the year 2000-2006, Chris Hoofnagle was a senior counsellor of the Electronic Privacy Information Center (EPIC), and according to him, credit reports were used to reject opportunities for a loan and other services. Consumers were also not allowed to view their credit scores back then, and that CRA's would only report the negative and unnecessary information about the consumer. The reports would include political views, lifestyle, sexual orientation, and etcetera.

Because of this irregularity among the CRA's, a major congressional inquiry took place in 1971, where FCRA or the Fair Credit Reporting Act was conceded by the Congress. This inquiry created a structure of correct, accurate and fair credit reporting. The act promoted fair information practices that secure a consumer's privacy and information, allowing them to view, correct and dispute any wrong information about their accounts.

In 2001, consumers are finally able to get direct access to their credit score. The amended version signed by previous President George W. Bush in December 2003 required CRA's to give consumers at a reasonable price. These days, there are many ways to get your hands on your credit scores, and we will provide links at the later part of this book.

What Are Credit Scores?

Just when you thought getting scores is far behind you from when you were still in school, think again. As an adult, Credit Scores most of the time is what can make or break you, in terms of getting a new car or a new house.

Credit scores are the determining factor for banks and credit unions as to whether or not they will take the risk of lending you money or services. It is a three digit number produced by a mathematical algorithm using information in your credit report. It's intended to predict risk, and more specifically, the likelihood that you will become delinquent on your credit responsibilities within the next 24 months.

Aside from being used as basis for a loan or credit card approvals, credit scores are also now used by other agencies and companies for job applications and other services.

In determining your credit scores, a certain algorithm or mathematical formula is used, basically it is what is known as Predictive Analytics. They use certain information and analyse it to come up with a conclusion regarding a consumer's reliability when it comes to debt paying, and if they are able to handle a bigger credit line. The most commonly used is a formula that is developed by the Fair Isaac Co Company, or is now known as FICO. Another credit score source is the one from VantageScore. We will talk about these scorings more later.

What Is FICO?

FICO stands for Fair Isaac Co, a company that provides most of the credit scores that we know today. The company started in 1956 by Engineer Bill Fair and its Mathematician Earl Isaac. They launched ASAP, their very first automated application-processing system that debuted in Wells Fargo bank in 1971. Today, the term FICO is not just referring to the company, but to the mathematical formula that they use for analytics. There were different analytical algorithms developed that caters to different needs of each company who wants to get hold of a consumer's or an applicant's credit score. FICO also bases their scores from information gathered by the 3 major credit bureaus – Equifax, TransUnion and Experian - and from the information they gathered, they will use a certain formula to analyze a person's probability of being able to pay their debt on time or if they will get bankrupt in a few years' time.

What makes up your FICO scores?

In general, the FICO score range is from 300 to 850, the higher number signifying less risk to the lender or guarantor.

Consumers with outstanding FICO scores, about 760 or greater, are probable to get the best rates when they borrow, lesser interest, and the best discounts on insurance.

This pie chart shows what makes up your FICO score.

• 10% is based whether or not it is your first time to get a credit, or the number of inquiries that's been done to your credit history. We will talk more about credit inquiries later.

• 10% is based on the types of accounts you have had

• 15% is the age of your credit history. The longer your credit history is the better

• 30% is from the amount of debt you have

• 35% is the largest chunk, and this refers to your payment history – if you had any late payments or if you are always paying your bills on time

All of these aspects are also measured in other credit score models, so you can positively conclude that if you have a good solid FICO scor, the chances of you getting a high score in other credit scoring models are high. But, for some consumers, the weight of these categories can differ. For instance, people who haven't been using credit for a long time will be considered differently than those with a longer credit history, according to FICO. So, the significance of any one of these factors rest on the overall information in your credit report.

Following the amendments on the FCRA years ago, anything that is considered not related to your credit scores will not be included in your FICO scores. These unnecessary factors would be your personal beliefs, sexual orientation, political beliefs, and your personal information such as medical records, address and age.

FICO has many credit score models. Some of these models are specific to what the end user is applying for. If you are applying for an auto loan for example, your potential creditor may use a FICO score formula that gives significant weight to your history of making auto loan payments. Other models are modified for FICO's clients' specific needs.

Furthermore, FICO modernizes its common formulas from time to time, with the most recent being the FICO 9 rollout in 2014. Paid collection accounts are not incorporated into FICO 9 scores, and owed medical collections have lesser negative impact on credit scores, compared to other credit scoring models and former FICO algorithms.

What is VantageScore

Just like FICO, VantageScore is another type of credit scoring system. It started in 2006 through a mutual program agreement of the three major credit bureaus – Equifax, TransUnion and Experian. It is also considered as second in the most trusted credit scoring systems after FICO.

The latest version of VantageScore, the VantageScore 3.0 launched in March 2013, not only delivers scores to general users but also helps about 30 to 35 million people who may not have a credit profile with other models, whether because they are first timers in doing credit, or just don't use credit that frequently.

What makes up your Vantagescore scores?

Corresponding to other credit scores, your Vantage score entails of calculations that depend entirely on credit bureau information — not income, bank accounts or other assets — to predict how likely you are to pay your debt obligations monthly in a timely manner. Your scores are affected by your practice of paying on time, keeping debt balances low when it comes to your total credit limits, the age of your credit accounts and its variety and the number of inquiries on your credit reports.

The straightforwardness and common sense of credit scores are often tainted by numerous credit reporting errors that can lead to credit scoring problems, and so it is a must that you closely monitor your scores. There are many ways to check your credit scores.

A quick comparison between scorings of FICO and VantageScore

Once your chosen scoring model is done with their analytical calculations about your reliability, you will be presented with your very own 3-digit score. On the figure above, you should be able to see the comparison between FICO scoring and VantageScore point system.

Rating	FICO	VANTAGESCORE
Exceptional / Excellent	800 – 850	750 – 850
Very Good / Good	740 – 799	700 – 749
Good / Fair	670 – 739	650 – 699
Fair / Poor	580 – 669	550 – 649

Very Poor	300 – 579	300 - 549

I can say that compared to the FICO scores, Vantage gives an extreme-to-extreme scoring. The range of scores that they give for the Excellent and Very Poor fields are quiet wider than those of FICO's. The wider range from Vantage though would be the Poor field, whereas on the FICO pie, the ranges are somewhat equal to each other.

It is a wrong assumption that Vantage gives more emphasis on the negative scores just so an applicant for loan or credit card would get rejected because of the ranges of scores that they offer. However, it would be safe to say that these scorings are not at all that accurate – there are still some discrepancies that you can always dispute and have corrected should the need arise.

Chapter 3: The Inner Workings Of Your

Credit Score

There is a very simple formula that can be used to help you understand your FICO credit score. Fair Isaac Corporation (FICO) is the scoring system designed that most creditors will use when making a lending decision. Each section of your credit represents a certain percentage as to how you are scored. Here are the factors involved.

How your score is calculated based on the following percentages:

1) 35% is your **Payment History**- this section represents your history of making payments on all credit accounts.

2) 30% is the **Amount Owed**- this is this most important section of your score that will allow you to generate the quickest boost to your score. It takes into account all limits of credit lines you have available and compares it to the amount owed.

(This section can account for 100+ points of your credit score)

3) 15% is the **Length of Credit Accounts**-Your FICO score takes into consideration your oldest active account and averages the age of all accounts.

4) 10% **New Credit**- This section takes into account all new accounts opened and inquires for new credit. This does not include your personal credit pulls. Also, to allow for you to shop for the best interest rate on a purchase, multiple inquires over a 14 day period will only count as one inquiry.

5) 10% **Credit in Use**- all credit accounts are considered

There are about 60 percent of people that have over a 700 credit score. If you have a 720 or better score, there is no need to raise it because lenders lump you into the same category as people with an 820. At that point you are viewed as a safe risk.

However, **if you are below a 720** it is worth trying these few tricks outlined in this book to increase your score. It could save you thousands of dollars on interest alone.

Chapter 4: Credit Reports

Step1: I Got My Credit Report For Free Every Year and Reviewed It Carefully

In the United States, you can get a copy of your credit report from the three main credit bureaus for free every year. This is something I still do **every year**.

Reminder tip: I set an annual date on my calendar to remind me to obtain my credit reports and this reminder automatically repeats every year. It's very helpful.

There are a lot of websites and services that offer "Free Credit Reports" but come attached to all kinds of other offers and services that you'll need to pay for and don't really need.

I only use **AnnualCreditReport.com** to request my credit reports, because it is reputable and there are no hidden offers or fees. If you're interested in doing this, you can go to the website and follow the steps for obtaining your free credit report **for all three credit bureaus**. It's important to obtain your credit report from all three bureaus because each one of them contains slightly different information.

If you visit **AnnualCreditReport.com**, be sure you give yourself plenty of time to complete the process of requesting your credit report from all three bureau websites. A couple of hours at least is good. Remember: patience and perseverance.

You'll need to create an account for each bureau, and they will ask you for information that only you would know to verify your identity online. If your identity can be verified online, you'll have access to your credit report online right then and there.

I strongly recommend printing a hard copy of your credit report or saving an electronic copy before moving onto the next credit bureau, so you have access to it in the future. You'll be able to track your progress by reviewing your old credit reports.

Once I have my three credit reports, I carefully read them **line by line** and make that I understand every piece of information that is included in the reports. If I don't understand something, I investigate. There should be company phone numbers listed for any accounts that are open or closed and I use those numbers to call for more information.

Sometimes mistaken identity or fraud can be the cause of a problem on someone's credit report. I always check to see that all of the items listed on my credit report are indeed mine. Because I print the credit reports out on paper, I can circle or highlight errors and make notes about what steps I've taken to correct them and what steps I'd like to do next. I look for addresses that I've never lived at, loans that don't belong to me, late payments that aren't accurate, etc. I'm looking for anything that doesn't look right.

(If you suspect some type of fraud or identity theft, you can place a security freeze on your credit report to stop anyone from accessing your credit report or opening accounts in your name. This is a significant step and often challenging to undo, so be sure to research exactly what this means on the websites of each credit bureau.)

On a credit report, there are sections for positive items, negative items, any judgments or liens, previous addresses and inquiries, etc. Understanding all of the information included in these sections is important. Remember: diligence.

If someone's identity cannot be verified online to the credit bureau's satisfaction, that person will need to submit a hardcopy paper request by mail. I know this may sound tedious and boring, but I recommend taking the time to do it. It's important, and if someone's truly serious about raising their credit score, they'll be sure to complete this step. The credit bureaus will have a hardcopy document to download and print on their website and instructions for how to send the request in by mail. All three credit bureaus may also take requests online via their website. Here are the three main credit bureaus and their contact information if needed:

Equifax
equifax.com
PO Box 105069
Atlanta, GA 30349
(800) 525-6285

Experian
experian.com

TransUnion
transunion.com
PO Box 6790
Fullerton, CA 92634
(800) 680-7289

Disputing Information On A Credit Report

Mistakes to credit reports do happen! I dispute any inaccurate information that is on my credit report. This may seem like a tedious thing to do and will take some time to accomplish, but it's worth it if there's something that isn't accurate on the credit report. All three credit bureaus accept disputes online. The procedures are on their websites.

In addition, there is also a step-by-step process on the Federal Trade Commission's website, which includes a sample letter that is downloadable as a template. Here is the link: **http://www.consumer.ftc.gov/articles/0151-disputing-errors-credit-reports**.

Chapter 5: The Fact That Finally Fixes

Your Credit

The next set of words that you are going to read will uncover a truth that has been present from your birth, but the full understanding of it may not occur until now. In my years of counseling, this one fact I have found, not only helps people fix their credit, but more importantly their overall lives...

The underlying truth is, "The best person, to understand and overcome the overall problem, is the person that created the problem." Many people will seek out help from a psychologist with problems that they already have the foundational answer. Over the years, I have uncovered that the most difficult emotion to overcome as it pertains to life is denial.

The Webster Dictionary defines Denial as:

A condition, in which someone will not admit that something sad, painful, etc., is true or real.

Denial is a very powerful emotion because if not dealt with upfront, any process attempted, is doomed to fail.

Denial is a very common feeling, especially when it comes to dealing with life's negative experiences and adverse circumstances. In the case of credit, when a person reflects on their lower than standard credit score and unstable financial status, words such as stress and depression tend to arise. The primary reason the thought of credit is so stressful is because it can result in you getting approved or declined for a car loan to get you to work and even a house to have a roof over your head. The problem is that no one wants to get declined in life and when a human naturally gets rejected there is an instant temptation to become depressed. To avoid that result, they frantically find ways to deny it, and then frivolously find someone else to deal with it entirely.

In essence, no one likes to promote their credit score if it is low. The reason is simple; your credit report reveals the timeline of life's events. A lower credit score indirectly exhibits failure. Your credit score is a snapshot of your life's history; however, the people looking at your credit report and score will not be able to comprehend the full story.

With the above in mind, the first person that you need to forgive, is yourself. You are the person that went through it, and you are the only one that has the ability to ultimately overcome it. The first thing to do is identify how the event(s) came about and if it could have been avoidable.

Some life's events could have been preventable while others could not. The truth is that a death or a hindrance to one's health that stops the ability to obtain income probably is unavoidable. However, an avoidable situation is one in which you purchased that brand new car when you knew you could not really afford it because your student loans were coming out of deferment a few months later!

When asked, "Why did you purchase the car?" – One explains, "I bought the car because I work hard, and I deserve it."

This above statement confirms the quote, "Your life is a sum of all your individual choices."

At the end of the day, the person ultimately responsible for this process being successful is the person who is reading this book. You are the best person for the job and actually, the expert, because you understand all the ends and outs of how the negative credit items came about.

Thus, not only are you the best person to "face" the problem, but also the best person to "fix" the problem.

In order to break down any doubts, I want to take the time to dispel all myths that it might be better for you to go to a Debt Settlement Company to fix your current problems. Not only is this not wise, but I want to shed some light on the industry so you can discover this for yourself.

Top three reasons why Debt Settlement Companies are not the best option:

Reason #1 – Some Creditors refuse to work with Debt Settlement Companies: There are some Creditors who refuse to work with Debt Settlement Companies. Since they won't work with them, it may cause your accounts to go further delinquent than needed. When the Original Creditor refuses to cooperate with a Debt Settlement Company in regards to your debt, Debt Settlement Companies will wait for it to go to a collection company. This strategy causes you to miss out on great settlement opportunities. When you decide to settle your accounts yourself, you don't have to worry about the process being prolonged which can further mess up your credit in a very negative way.

Reason #2 – Debt Settlement Companies can be costing you more money: More times than not, when you deal directly with a Creditor you are more likely to strike a better deal overall. This previous statement is true by the very structure of Debt Settlement Companies. The process is that you agree to put a certain amount of money in a "special account" or escrow each month until you have enough money to pay off a settlement offer in full. However, if you were to go directly to the Creditor, you would be able to work out more flexible terms and payment arrangements than a Debt Settlement Company can. The hard truth is that it could be costing you almost 10% more by going with them.

Reason #3 - The Debt Settlement Company's fees stop you from paying the debt off faster: Majority of Debt Settlement Companies charges an estimated 22% of the enrolled debt as their fee structure. For example, if you went to a Debt Settlement Company with $30,000 in debt they would charge you an estimated 22% or $6,600 paid over time. The second fee structure of Debt Settlement Companies is the option of charging you a percentage of your total savings.For example, if they were able to set up a settlement offer that saved you $2,000, then they would take a percentage of that savings. Even though it might not sound bad, some companies have charged as high as 50% of a client's savings. Astonishingly, their fee structure is the primary way they make a profit. When you do it yourself, you could take that same savings and use it to pay your debts much more quickly.

In conclusion, hundreds of companies would love for you to ask them to do what you could do yourself. This book is just to remind lo one simple principle – **You are the best person for the job!!!**

Points to remember:

*The best person to "face" the problem is also the best person to "fix" the problem – that is you!!!

*Until you have overcome the mental battle, there can be no real victory.

The following chapter will assist you in building confidence as you get ready to deal with what you really owe. I will equip you with the knowledge of how each party of the collection process gets paid so you will comprehend the settlement strategy of, "How low, can you go?"

Chapter 6: Dispute The Charges

You should always keep an eye on your credit report. There are plenty of credit card companies and even websites that will provide it to you completely free so make sure you're taking advantage of that feature. You'll be able to monitor if someone ever steals your identity and you're also going to be able to keep track of the accounts that are affecting your credit score both in positive and negative ways.

If you look at your credit report and see a lot of negative accounts, such as past due or collection accounts, consider whether they are accurate. Did you know that the credit reporting agencies are required by law to ensure that your credit report is 100% accurate at all times? If it's not they are required (also by law) to remove the incorrect information.

What this means to you is that, if the negative accounts on your credit report are not 100% accurate you can request to have them removed. What you want to do is review your report and consider which accounts may not be correct. Now keep in mind you're not allowed to dispute anything that is true. So if the negative account on your credit report is accurate you're supposed to leave it alone. If it's not, write a letter to the credit reporting agency (that's Transunion, Equifax or Experian) and ask them to remove it. Let them know why it needs to be removed and make sure you include your name, birthdate and social security number in the letter.

If you do this then the credit reporting agency is required to investigate and make sure the account is accurate. If it is then they will send you a letter verifying the account and request that if you have evidence that it's not accurate you send that information to them. If it is not accurate they must remove it from your credit report and your credit score will be updated to reflect it.

Writing letters to the credit reporting agencies doesn't always work 100%. Sometimes they will continue to tell you an account has been verified when you know it isn't accurate. If this happens you'll have to go above their heads and write to the original creditor, letting them know that the account is inaccurate and providing information that verifies this. This could be statements showing your bills were paid on time or letters indicating that they removed the account. Remember to send copies of these documents and not the actual letter.

Disputing false information can get a lot of accounts dropped and it can remove some of your debt because you won't have to pay for those collections or past due charges if you can prove that they are not accurate. Plus this is going to improve your credit score and repair your credit because the negative accounts are being removed.

Chapter 7: What Is Your Credit Score?

Credit scores to some people are a scary monster they are forced to face every time they need their credit. Even though these people know in some way it's related to their creditworthiness; it's still intimidating or costly dealing with their credit. Your credit score however is not as scary as it may seem, and in fact can help just as much as it can hurt. The difference between good and bad credit is not as simple as whether you are approved or declined; but also what interest rate you are borrowing money at. Starting good credit habits is important so when you need your credit it will no longer be a scary monster, but a known factor that you benefit from.

Why do credit scores exist?

Credit scores serve as a reference for what borrowers are risky when it comes to lending money. In a perfect world everyone would pay back the debts they take on, but unfortunately that's not the case. So credit reports are kept and calculated to help companies make sound decisions when it comes to lending money. Because of this, your credit report could be your best friend or worst enemy. For anyone who has ever viewed their report, the raw data can be overwhelming to say the least. So who is responsible for this information that has the potential to affect your life so much? There are actually three credit bureaus: Equifax, TransUnion, and Experian; and each keep track of all credit information reported about you. This can range from credit cards, to a long lost phone bill that was never paid. When it comes down to it, you better believe if you owe any company money they are reporting it to the bureaus. A complicated system is used to incorporate all this information to spew out a score between 350 and 950. The reason it can become complicated is that two people could have very similar information and could still have very different scores. Below are some key terms that deal with your credit card and credit report, they will help you understand the topics covered in this guide.

Terms to know

Billing Cycle- Billing cycles are the opening and closing dates of your credit card statements. These directly correlate to your due date and what charges show on which statements.

Revolving Balance- A revolving balance refers to any balance that carries month to month. Let's say you have a credit card that the first of every month you buy 300 dollars worth of groceries, and at the end of the month pay it off completely. For this example you would have a revolving balance of zero. Now if you paid only 200 of the 300 dollars off you would now have a 100 dollar revolving balance.

Inquiry- Any time you apply for credit or look at your own credit report, it places an inquiry on it. Creditors generally see high inquiries as a negative sign, and can bring down your score.

Charged off- This refers to a credit card that stops receiving payment and the company has written the debt off, sometimes debt owed is sold to collection agencies.

Current Household Income- on most credit applications this will be found, and is asking for the annual income of everyone living in the same residence as you.

APR- The annual percentage rate is used to calculate finance charges, which is the money paid each month in interest.

What factors determine a healthy credit score?

Your credit report can be affected by many other things besides credit cards (medical bills, mortgages, and car loans to name a few). Keep this in mind when viewing these factors, as they may help with any aspect of credit but are geared towards your credit cards. For example a car loan may not be applicable for debt to limit ratio.

Credit history depth

If you are new to credit this will probably be a major reason you are declined credit. This is the amount of time you have had credit reporting. So if you are fresh out the gate, you may get declined just because there is not enough information to base a decision off of. The longer your credit history, the more accurate and solid the overall information provided is.

How to Improve: Allow your credit to build over time, and be aware of how much credit history you have. For this a credit report doesn't need to be pulled, just think back to whenever the first loan or credit card you had was.

Keep in Mind: A good credit history has multiple credit information reporting for a long time. Say you have one credit card that was opened ten years ago and four others five years ago. Someone looking at the report may not consider the depth of the report accurate because there is only one piece of information reporting for that long.

Late payments

The first basic rule everyone knows about credit is to make your payments on time. This point is very valid, but there are some things you may not know about how it actually works. For example some companies won't report a late payment until it is 30 days delinquent (there still are some that will report after one day). So next time you are late and worried it's going to ding your score, give the company a call and ask when they report.

How to Improve: We are all human and can have that "Oops" moment where a payment is missed. The best way to cover your bases is to set up auto payment **through** your credit provider. I stress this because most credit cards have a bill cycle that correlates with the due date, which is something that can (rarely) change. Auto payment through the credit provider will adjust if your due date changes, which is not the case through a third party.

Keep in Mind: That even if a late payment doesn't get reported that it still can cause your APR to increase as well as a late fee. It is always going to be best to make payments on time, but if it happens call your credit provider. It never hurts to try to get fees waived or APRs lowered.

Debt to Limit ratio

Out of all the factors listed, this is one of the most impacting. What this is referring to is how much overall debt are revolving balances compared to your total credit limits. Let's say Johnny owes $500 total on three credit cards and his combined credit limits are $1000. This calculates out to 50% usage. Some of the reasons this information is so impacting is because unlike other aspects of your report, this is in the now. If someone has a high percentage, it means they are struggling with what is currently available to them. So obviously the best is to have 0% right? But this actually is wrong, and is almost as bad as using credit too much. Think of it this way, you are a business trying to decide if you should lend someone money. When you see a credit report that has no use of credit it tells you two things. For one it says this person is not using what they have, which means they may not be that profitable. The second is they do not have any experience with dealing with a credit balance. Ideally you want someone who shows they can handle a balance with a due bill every month, but not so much that they are over their heads.

How to Improve: A good goal for this is to use 40% of what's available to you. The best way to manage this with a credit card is to calculate 40% of the limit and make a purchase that is slightly higher. If you set up auto payment, allow the minimum payment to be made until the balance drops a bit (how much is up to you, but I would say let half of the balance get paid off.) From here simply make another purchase to raise the balance again.

Keep in Mind: That the goal is to have an **overall** usage of 40%. If you have one card with a better APR, it may make more sense to shift more debt to this card. Just make sure to lessen debt on another so they balance out.

Chapter 8: The Basics

Before you start boosting your credit score, you need to know the basics. You need to know what a credit score is, how it is developed, and why it is important to you in your everyday life.

Lenders certainly know what sort of information they can get from a credit score, but knowing this information yourself can help you better see how your everyday financial decisions impact the financial picture lenders get of you through your credit score. A few simple tips are all you need to know to understand the basic principles: Tip #1: Understand where credit scores come from. If you are going to improve your credit score, then logic has it that you must understand what your credit score is and how it works. Without this information, you won't be able to very effectively improve your score because you won't understand how the things you do in daily life affect your score.

If you don't understand how your credit score works, you will also be at the mercy of any company that tries to tell you how you can improve your score - on their terms and at their price.

In general, your credit score is a number that lets lenders know how much of a credit risk you are. The credit score is a number, usually between 300 and 850, that lets lenders know how well you are paying off your debts and how much of a credit risk you are.

In general, the higher your credit score, the better credit risk you make and the more likely you are to be given credit at great rates. Scores in the low 600s and below will often give you trouble in finding credit, while scores of 720 and above will generally give you the best interest rates out there. However, credit scores are a lot like GPAs or SAT scores from college days - while they give others a quick snapshot of how you are doing, they are interpreted by people in different ways. Some lenders put more emphasis on credit scores than others.

Some lenders will work with you if you have credit scores in the 600s, while others offer their best rates only to those creditors with very high scores indeed. Some lenders will look at your entire credit report while others will accept or reject your loan application based solely on your credit score.

The credit score is based on your credit report, which contains a history of your past debts and repayments. Credit bureaus use computers and mathematical calculations to arrive at a credit score from the information contained in your credit report.

Each credit bureau uses different methods to do this (which is why you will have different scores with different companies) but most credit bureaus use the FICO system. FICO is an acronym for the credit score calculating software offered by Fair Isaac Corporation company. This is by far the most used software since the Fair

Isaac Corporation developed the credit score model used by many in the financial industry and is still considered one of the leaders in the field.

In fact, credit scores are sometimes called FICO scores or FICO ratings, although it is important to understand that your score may be tabulated using different software.

One other thing you may want to understand about the software and mathematics that goes into your credit score is the fact that the math used by the software is based on research and comparative mathematics. This is an important and simple concept that can help you understand how to boost your credit score. In simple terms, what this means is that your credit score is in a way calculated on the same principles as your insurance premiums.

Your insurance company likely asks you questions about your health, your lifestyle choices (such as whether you are a smoker) because these bits of information can tell the insurance company how much of a risk you are and how likely you are to make large claims later on. This is based on research.

Studies have shown, for example, that smokers tend to be more prone to serious illnesses and so require more medical attention. If you are a smoker, you may face higher insurance premiums because of this.

Similarly, credit bureaus and lenders often look at general patterns. Since people with too many debts tend not to have great rates of repayment, your credit score may suffer if you have too many debts, for example. Understanding this can help you in two ways:

1) It will let you see that your credit score is not a personal reflection of how "good" or "bad" you are with money. Rather, it is a reflection of how well lenders and companies think you will repay your bills - based on information gathered from studying other people.

2) It will let you see that if you want to improve your credit score, you need to

work on becoming the sort of debtor that studies have shown tends to repay their bills. You do not have to work hard to reinvent yourself financially and you do not have to start making much more money. You just need to be a reliable lender. This realization alone should help make credit repair far less stressful!

Credit reports are put together by credit bureaus, which use information from client companies. It works like this: credit bureaus have clients - such as credit card companies and utility companies, to name just two - who provide them with information.

Once a file is begun on you (i.e. once you open a bank account or have bills to pay) then information about you is stored on the record. If you are late paying a bill, the clients call the credit bureaus and note this. Any unpaid bills, overdue bills or other problems with credit count as "dings" on your credit report and affect your score.

Information such as what type of debt you have, how much debt you have, how regularly you pay your bills on time, and your credit accounts are all information that is used to calculate your credit score.

Your age, sex, and income do not count towards your credit score. The actual formula used by credit bureaus to calculate credit scores is a well-kept secret, but it is known that recent account activity, debts, length of credit, unpaid accounts, and types of credit are among the things that count the most in tabulating credit scores from a credit report.

Tip #2: Keep the contact information for credit bureaus handy. The three major credit bureaus are important to contact if you are going to be repairing your credit score. The major three credit agencies can help you by sending you your credit report. If you find an error on your credit report, these are also the companies you must contact in order to correct the problem. You can easily contact these organizations by mail, telephone, or through the Internet:

Equifax Credit Information Services, Inc Address: P.O. Box 740241 Atlanta, GA 30374 Telephone: 1-888-766-0008 Online: www.equifax.com

TransUnion LLC Consumer Disclosure Center

Address: P.O. Box 1000 Chester, PA 19022 Telephone: 1_800_888_4213 Online: www.tuc.com

Experian National Consumer Assistance Center Address: PO Box 2002 Allen, TX 75013 Telephone:1-888-397-3742 Online: www.experian.com

You may want to note this information wherever most of your financial information is kept so that you can easily contact the bureaus whenever you need to. Your local yellow pages should also have the contact information of these credit agencies as well.

Tip #3: Develop an action plan for dealing with your credit score. Once you have your credit report and your credit score, you will be able to tell where you stand and where many of your problems lie. If you have a poor score, try to see in your credit report what could be causing the problem:

-Do you have too much debt? -Too many unpaid bills? -Have you recently faced a major financial upset such as a bankruptcy? -Have you simply not had credit long enough to establish good credit? -Have you defaulted on a loan, failed to pay taxes, or recently been reported to a collection agency?

The problems that contribute to your credit problems should dictate how you decide to boost your credit score. As you read through this ebook, highlight or jot down those tips that apply to you and from them develop a checklist of things you can do that would help your credit situation improve.

When you seek professional credit counseling or credit help, counselors will generally work with you to help you develop a personalized strategy that expressly addresses your credit problems and financial history. Now, with this ebook, you can develop a similar strategy on your own - in your own time and at your own cost.

When developing your action plan, know where most of your credit score is coming from:

1) Your credit history (accounts for more than a third of your credit score in some cases). Whether or not you have been a good credit risk in the past is considered the best indicator of how you will react to debt in the future. For this reason, late payment, loan defaults, unpaid taxes, bankruptcies, and other unmet debt responsibilities will count against you the most. You can't do much about your financial past now, but starting to pay your bills on time - starting today - can help boost your credit score in the future.

2) Your current debts (accounts for approximately a third of your credit score in some cases). If you have lots of current debt, it may indicate that you are

stretching yourself financially thin and so will have trouble paying back debts in the future. If you have a lot of money owing right now - and especially if you have borrowed a great deal recently - this fact will bring down your credit score. You an boost your credit score by paying down your debts as far as you can.

3) How long you have had credit (accounts for up to 15% of your credit score in some cases). If you have not had credit accounts for very long, you may not have enough of a history to let lenders know whether you make a good credit risk. Not having had credit for a long time can affect your credit score. You can counter this by keeping your accounts open rather than closing them off as you pay them off.

4) The types of credit you have (accounts for about one tenth of your credit score, in most cases). Lenders like to see a mix of financial responsibilities that you handle well. Having bills that you pay as well as one or two types of loans can actually

improve your credit score. Having at least one credit card that you manage well can also help your credit score.

As you can see, it is possible to only estimate how much a specific area of your credit report affects your credit score. Nevertheless, keeping these five areas in mind and making sure that each is addressed in your personalized plan will go a long way in making sure that your personalized credit repair plan is comprehensive enough to boost your credit effectively.

The Best Ways to Boost Your Credit Score Because of the way credit scores are calculated, some actions you take will affect your credit score better than others. In general, paying your bills on time and meeting your financial responsibilities will boost your score the most. Owing a reasonable amount of money and being able to repay it will show lenders that you take your finances seriously and pose little threat of lost money. There are a few tips that, more than any other, will boost your credit score the most:

Tip # 4: Pay your bills on time. One of the best ways to improve your credit score is simply to pay your bills on time. This is absurdly simple but it works very well, because nothing shows lenders that you take debts seriously as much as a history of paying promptly. Every lender wants to be paid in full and on time.

If you pay all your bills on time then the odds are good that you will make the payments on a new debt on time, too, and that is certainly something every lender wants to see. Experts think that up to 35% of your credit score is based on your paying of bills on time, so this simple step is one of the easiest ways to boost your credit score.

Paying your bills on time also ensures that you don't get hit with late fees and other financial penalties that make paying your bills off harder. Paying your bills in a timely way makes it easier to keep making payments on time.

Of course, if you have had problems making your payments on time in the past, your current credit score will reflect this. It will take a number of months of repaying your bills on time to improve your credit score again, but the effort will be well worth it when your credit risk rating rebounds!

Tip #5: Avoid excessive credit. If you have many lines of credit or several huge debts, you make a worse credit risk because you are close to "overextending your credit." This simply means that you may be taking on more credit than you can comfortably pay off. Even if you are making payments regularly now on existing bills, lenders know that you will have a harder time paying off your bills if your debt load grows too much.

The higher your debts the greater your monthly debt payments and so the higher the risk that you will eventually be able to repay your debts. Plus, statistical studies have shown that those with high debt loads have the hardest time financially when faced with a crisis such as a divorce, unemployment, or sudden illness.

Lenders (and credit bureaus who calculate your credit score) know that the more debt you have the greater problems you will have in case you do run into a life crisis.

In order to have a great credit score, avoid taking out excessive credit. You should stick to one or two credit cards and one or two other major debts (car loan, mortgage) in order to have the best credit rating. Do not apply for every new credit line or credit card "just in case." Borrow only when you need it and make sure to make payments on your debts on time.

You should also know that taking out lots of new credit accounts in a relatively short period of time will cause your credit score to nosedive because it will look as though you are being financially irresponsible.

Tip #6: Pay Down Your Debts If you have a lot of debt, your credit score will suffer. Paying down your debts to a minimum will help elevate your credit score. For example, if you have a $1000 limit on your credit card and you regularly carry a balance of $900, you will be a less attractive credit risk to lenders than someone who has the same credit card but carries a smaller balance of $100 or so. If you are serious about improving your credit score, then start with the largest debt you have and start paying it down so that you are using a less large percentage of your credit total.

In general, try to make sure that you use no more than 50% of your credit. That means that if your credit card has a limit of $5000, make sure that you pay it down to at least $2500 and work at carrying no larger balance. If possible, reduce the debt even more. If you can pay off your credit card in full each month, that is even better. What counts here is what percentage of your total credit limit you are using - the lower the better.

Tip #7: Have a range of credit types. The types of credit you have are a factor in calculating your credit score. In general, lenders like to see that you are able to handle a range of credit types well. Having some form of personal credit - such as credit cards - and some larger types of credit - such as a mortgage or auto loan - and paying them off regularly is better than having only one type of credit.

Chapter 9: Understanding Your Credit

Report

Your credit report is the single most important document for your financial life. The report may seem relatively trivial to you as it only contains information that you may already know personal data, credit history and accounts. However, for other, especially your potential creditors, each entry can mean the approval or disapproval of your loan application.

The compilation of this information is made possible because of the credit bureau. Take note, while you may have a mortgage account in Bank A, a credit card in Bank B or a loan in Lending Institution C, all these information from each of your respective banks and financial institutions are stored in a credit bureau. This is made possible because every time you fill out a form applying for a credit card, a loan or any instrument for credit, the form is sent to the bureau. Your personal data is used to match the application form with any other form or information that is already in file in the bureau.

The credit report is also called credit history or credit score in other countries but they all contain the same type of information. Regardless of what it is called, it is essentially your financial reputation. You may think that such personal or private information remain confidential and known only to you and to your banks. However, the credit report has another purpose aside as a documentation of all your financial information.

Whenever you apply for another credit instrument, for example a credit card or a loan, the bank or financing institution will request your credit report from the credit bureau. They will use the report as a tool to evaluate your qualification for your application. For example, they can measure if you are a good payer of debt if you are always on time on your payments.

You may be overwhelmed on the information, words, dates, figures and numbers on your credit report. There are generally four categories from which all information in the credit report belongs. These are:

1. Personal information and it contains:

a.Your name and other aliases that you may have used

b.Your current and previous addresses

c. Your date of birth

d.Your social security number

e.Your current and previous employment

2.Public information and it contains:

a.Liens

b.Judgments

c. Bankruptcies

d.Wage garnishments

e.Other open legal issues that have yet to be resolved

3.Creditor information and it contains:

a.Accounts, whether closed, open or current or charged off

b.Ownership of the account, whether individual or joint

c. The balance of the loan

d.The last payment made on the loan

e.Terms of the loan

f. Credit limit

g.Adverse account information and it contains information about loans with which you have late payments, remaining balance and any other account that has been forwarded to a collection agency. The information in this category generally hurt your credit reputation.

h.Any other information pertaining to your payment performance

4.Credit inquiries and it contains:

a.Hard inquiries, these are made by lenders who requested for your credit report to assess any application you may have made. The name of the bank, address, and phone number will be listed as an inquirer. Usually, if you have applied for a loan for example, the name of the bank or financial institution will appear in this section.

Soft inquiries, these are made either by you or pre-approved products made by marketing agencies of credit card companies and other lenders.

Chapter 10: Empowerment

What is the life you would choose for yourself? Would it be a life of travel and luxury? Would it be a simple life with a garden and many friends? Perhaps you would volunteer more time and money to that cause which makes your heart break and swell all at once.

Whatever that life is, it is fully within your ability to achieve.

Many doubt that last statement, especially those who are in a battle with their finances. The persistent nagging of financial woes leaves us harboring feelings of incompetence. We question our value. We doubt our abilities. We box up our dreams so we don't have to face them in the midst of our struggles.

But your dreams are are achievable. You are capable and competent. You are unique, and for that reason alone, among many others, you are of extraordinary value.

While it is absolutely true that money is not the goal of our existence, financial strife in today's world makes it exceedingly difficult to move forward. Developing empowering financial habits is only partially about our finances. It is also about setting the stage to build an intentional life.

But what is the role of credit in all this? And what is meant by "credit friendly?"

Credit serves two purposes: as both a measurement and a key.

As a measurement, credit scores are designed to assess one's willingness and ability to repay his or her obligations as agreed. In this role credit acts as a meaningful measure of financial empowerment. When we begin to lose control of our financial lives, the evidence is likely to show up in the management of our balances and in our ability to pay on time. As a result, our scores are likely to drop, reflecting the challenges we face. On the other hand, as we become more financially empowered our credit scores rise.

Credit is also a key. Solid credit opens doors to financial tools that further empower us. Poor credit locks those doors, making it that much harder for us to move in positive directions.

"Credit friendly" is simply a term reflecting that the habits shared in this book are not only financially empowering but should also have a positive impact on your credit scores. Not every seemingly logical financial strategy leads to better credit. For example, closing old accounts and becoming 'debt free' are two very popular and understandable financial strategies which can, unfortunately, lead to lower credit scores.

Yet the cost of poor credit cannot be ignored. In addition to the problem of access to financial tools, poor credit results in higher interest rates on all credit products, meaning higher costs for our purchases. Poor credit raises our insurance rates and impacts our ability to get work.

As financially prudent as going debt-free may seem, the wider use of credit demands that we learn the habits of credit friendly financial management and stay in the game.

Where are you on the financial empowerment continuum?

Empowerment, is the quality of having control, to be able to put something to its best and highest use. Financial empowerment is simply that quality in our financial lives. At one end of the continuum is the domain of tax liens and collections, of financial dis-empowerment. At this end, one's ability to use money for any chosen purpose is all but gone.

At the other end our financial resources are able to be used fully for any purpose. At this end, all the habits of financial empowerment are fully integrated. We are protected from unexpected turns in our financial state. We are free to design our life and to invest in ourselves.

Each of us lies somewhere between these two extremes. **To move toward the empowered end is our goal.**

In the following chapters are a collection of 10 financial habits assembled during my banking years and bolstered by continuing study in the fields of appreciative inquiry and communication. Awareness, planning and action are all integrated in a thorough, yet accessible, system to become more financially empowered. By incorporating these habits into your own life you position yourself to thrive.

Chapter 11: Credit card

balances

So one of the credit corrections you need to make is your Credit card balances 30% or below (great) to improve credit scores. 30%-60% (neutral) does not really effect it positively or negatively. 60% + (hurting credit score) a quick way to effect this is to either pay your balances down under 30% of your balance or ask for more credit: for example if you have a $500.00 limit take it up
$1000.00 limit and nothing has to change in your lifestyle at all just your percentage of Debt to credit ratio is under 30% of your balance. Another credit approach is to open a secured credit card walk into your bank and ask for example a $500.00 secured credit line and actually give them $500.00 they are gonna give you a card that you can spend up to $500.00 every

month and you pay yourself back every month easy and a simple way to build your credit right away. Those are 2 ways to build your credit score fast. **Also negotiate with your creditors they can often remove your bad credit with a click**

of the button most Visa, MasterCard, and gas companies have a direct link to the credit

bureau by coming to a agreement to pay the loan off for a reduce price of what the outstanding balance they just might take those bad marks off of your record, then call

the credit bureau and confirm to see if the bad credit has been cleared. Start Rebuilding process Ask a creditor for forgiveness If you have been a good customer for years, but had a rough stretch and missed a payment or was late a few times you might be able to ask your creditor to "erase" a negative listing. You can do this with a GOODWILL LETTER. There no guarantee that a lender will do this but

this method has had a lot of success(there will be a example of a goodwill letter in the book on later page). Dispute old negatives, say your insurance company never paid some medical bills and now have a collection accounts, you can continue protesting that the charge was unjust, or you can try disputing the account with credit bureau as "not mine". The older and smaller a collection account, the more likely
the collection agency won't have bothered to update, the system with correct information and the credit bureau won't be able to match up the computer records. Remove a debt from your report if you pay it this method is called "pay for delete" and it works like a charm or smaller amounts of $500.00 and under especially medical collection remember to get the agreement in writing before you pay them anything, and only send a money order after you get them to agree to settling your debts

Chapter 12: What Makes A Credit

Report/Score

A credit report is a statement that has information about your credit activity and current credit situation such as loan paying history and the status of your credit accounts. Your credit score is an automated number that uses algorithms to summarize your credit risk, based on a snapshot of your credit report at a particular point in time. So, for those of you that have less than perfect score, fear not! There are things you can do immediately that can have a positive impact on your score starting today. Your credit score tells creditors how able you are to pay back your debt over the next 2-3 years. Credit scores are like batting averages, not golf scores, so the higher the better. Higher credit scores equate to the best credit approval rates so you don't get denied to finance that new car, house, investment or business. The high credit score also equates to the best interest rates and the possibility of being extending unsecured credit, meaning there's no collateral that the lender can take back. It is worth noting that there are different types of credit scores out there with FICO® being the most common. Other credit scores include the VantageScore or PLUS Score®. Typical credit scores range from 300 to 850 with 850 being the very best.

Your credit score is a three-digit number generated by a mathematical algorithm using information in your credit report. It's designed to predict risk, specifically, the likelihood that you will become seriously delinquent on your credit obligations in the 24 months after scoring. There is a multitude of credit scoring models in existence, but there's one that dominates the market – the FICO credit score. According to myFICO.com, the consumer website for the FICO score developer, "90 percent of all financial institutions in the U.S. use FICO scores in their decision-making process." FICO scores range from 300 to 850, where a higher number indicates lower risk. Now, you may ask, "What's a good score?" A good score is between 700 and 750, anything above that is a great score and below that is a fair, poor and bad. A consumer has three FICO scores, one for each credit report provided by the three major credit bureaus: Equifax, Experian, and TransUnion. Unfortunately, consumers currently have access to only their Equifax and TransUnion FICO scores. Experian ended its agreement with myFICO.com in 2009.

The importance of maintaining a good credit score

Having a good credit score is important because it'll help you in receiving affordable rates and terms from lenders. A credit score is what a lender uses to decide on whether you are eligible for the credit you require. In addition to determining whether you're eligible for the credit, a credit score is also important in determining the terms at which you receive a loan. Credit scores are used by banks, car dealers and credit card companies. Ideally, with a good credit score, you'll be able to get the best interest rates when you borrow money. The amount of interest charged on your credit is directly affected by the credit scores you have. The higher the credit score, the better the interest rates. You'll stand a better chance of getting your loan approved. Having a bad history of delinquencies may limit your chances of approval of the loan applied. Bad credit history will discourage you from applying for a loan. Even when you apply for one, the chances of getting the loan are lower due to the bad history. You'll enjoy superior bargaining power. With a good credit score, you're in a position to bargain for better interest rates. This allows you the freedom to shop around until you get the lender that'll give you the best rates. If you have a poor score, however, only a few lenders will consider your credit application and none of them will be willing to budge on the terms of credit. You'll miss out on cashback rewards, airline miles, and other perks. Having a good credit score is important because it ensures that your borrowing limit is higher. Lenders will easily allow you to borrow more money because of a good credit score. They'll have faith that you'll pay back the money at the agreed time due to your history.

Why the factors of credit exist

The factors of credit exist to help gauge your credit score. Each of the six factors of credit affects your score differently, both directly and indirectly to help determine if you are trustworthy. With businesses, such as insurance companies, have recently have started to use credit scores to make decisions about you. Utility companies now check your credit before establishing new service in your name, and some employers check your credit history (but not your actual credit score) to decide whether to give you a job, a raise, or promotion. Protecting and building your credit is more important than ever, and how you handle the following six factors, you can make all the difference in determining your credit score. Now, do not be alarmed with all the talk about who looks at your credit score and what it really determines for your future. This book is to help you, not scare you. I had a low score in my first year of college, somewhere around 520, and now I have a 776 by self-educating and learning what determines my score. As much as I wish it would have worked overnight, this process does not happen overnight. It took me about three years.

Factor 1: Credit Card Utilization

This is a high impact factor, which means it's very important to your credit score! The lower the credit card utilization, the better. Lenders really like to see that you're not using too much of the credit available to you, but of course, use a little. The tip here is to keep your balances low. I had trouble with this with my first year of having a credit card, so it's okay to mess up and learn. Another trick is to ask for a credit limit increase, which will help keep your utilization low. Use caution though!

Don't think that an increase in your credit limit is an invitation to spend more. A general rule of thumb is to keep your utilization under 30% for good credit and under 10% for excellent credit. This means that if you have a total $10,000 credit card limit, you should carry no more than a $1,000 balance and the same if you have a $1,000 credit card limit, you should carry no more than a $100 balance to have excellent credit card utilization. See below for the utilization percentages. These percentages were already calculated by my banking institution to help me understand what the best credit card utilization percentage is for credit score success.

Utilization Percentages
Excellent 0-9%
Good Credit10-29%
Fair Credit30-49%
Poor Credit50-74%
Bad Credit75+%

Factor 2: Payment History

Payment History is also a high impact factor. Lenders look at this factor to determine how likely you will make future payments on time. A payment that is more than thirty days late constitutes a late payment and, believe it or not, one late payment could hurt your credit score. You also maybe be penalized with a fee, increasing your balance. I learned the hard way, by being a broke college student with almost no money to make payments on time for my credit card, my credit score dropped like a sack of potatoes but I learned that the credit report keeps track of payments that are 30, 60, 90 and 120 days late, so if you go beyond thirty days, go ahead and get a payment in so you don't get hit for a sixty day lateness, which looks even worse than a 30 lateness! The tip here is to set up automatic bill pay, so you're never late and your payments are on time. You will appreciate this tip once you stop thinking about making your payment on time, because it was already deducted on or before your scheduled due date of payment, or even set a reminder for yourself. (It is a game changer once implemented.)

Ranges

Excellent 100%

Good Credit99%

Fair Credit98%

Poor Credit97%

Bad Credit<97%

Factor 3: Derogatory Remarks

This is the last high impact factor with less derogatory marks being better. A derogatory mark on your credit report could include something like the aforementioned late payment, repossession, a debt going into collections or even bankruptcy. The general rule of thumb is that these derogatory marks can camp out on your report for up to seven years, you read that right seven years, so do what you can to avoid them at all cost. Again, establishing automatic bill pay or setting reminders in your calendar to make a payment are crucial to avoid these on your credit report.

Ranges
Excellent 0
Good Credit0-1
Fair Credit1
Poor Credit2-3
Bad Credit4+

Now let's say you have accumulated a few derogatory remarks, don't freak out because there is a way to dispute these remarks although they have the capability to camp on your report for seven years. You can dispute them by going to that credit reporting bureau's website to have it removed. Depending on where the remark came from you can visit either site belonging to Equifax, Experian, or TransUnion. They each have a form to fill out. Don't dread the form, the form is to dispute the remark. It's a multiple choice form (usually) with a few text boxes where you can type out what is going on and what you have done to fix the issue. It is quick, easy, and usually, a credit score saver from loss of points before your next billing cycle has occurred.

Factor 4: Age of Credit

The higher (or longer) credit history, the better. Lenders like to see that you have experience using credit. This isn't always fair to the young consumer out there but look at it from the lender perspective. Would you be more comfortable lending to someone approaching retirement that has an expansive credit history or someone who just graduated high school? It's a no-brainer. One thing consumers often do is close paid off cards or zero balance lines of credit. This isn't always the best method with regard to your credit score. You can actually improve your age of credit history over time by keeping your accounts open and in good standing. After all, it takes nearly a decade of history to be considered excellent in this regard!

Ranges
Excellent 9+ years
Good Credit7-8 years
Fair Credit5-6 years
Poor Credit2-4 years
Bad Credit<2 years

There aren't many tips here but something I found out recently by talking to a representative at my banking institution is that someone as young as sixteen can be added to a credit card as an authorized user. Now, you may not want to trust someone that young to use the credit card but the payment history and activity will begin to show on that teenager's credit report to help begin building their credit score. By the age of nineteen, that teenager's score is about three years old with some credit history, now isn't that pretty great to know?

Factor 5: Total Accounts

The total accounts are also important to lenders. This factor suggests that other lenders have trusted you before. When I first learned about this, my thinking was backward. I thought lenders would like to see fewer accounts, not more. However, lenders like to see several varying accounts, such as revolving, installment, and open accounts because of the behaviors that are associated with them.

Revolving credit accounts (like a credit card) have varying payments and anything you don't pay is carried over to the following month with an agreed-upon interest charge. Installment credit accounts (like an auto loan or home mortgage) are accounts that typically have fixed payments with balances that amortize on a fixed schedule over time. Open credit accounts (like utility payments or cell phone bills) are paid in full each month and don't carry over. These particular types of accounts rarely show up on a credit report unless you decide against paying the water bill or Verizon for all that data you mistakenly used last month. You can improve your credit score by adding another type of account, however, use caution. Think twice before adding an account just to improve your overall number of accounts. Sometimes it isn't worth the additional risk of taking on more debt.

Ranges
Excellent 21
Good Credit11-20

Fair Credit9-14

Poor Credit6-10

Bad Credit0-5

Factor 6: Hard Inquiries

The last factor is hard inquiries with fewer inquiries being better for your overall credit score. Hard inquiries hit your credit report when you apply for credit. Although they are unavoidable, try to avoid unnecessary hard inquiries because they stay on your credit report for 2 years. One trick to practice is to take advantage of pre-approved credit card offers instead of applying for them. Pre-approval means the credit company doesn't need to check your credit so you can avoid the hit. Buying a car or some household furniture and need financing? It's still okay to shop around for the best deal because multiple inquiries in a short period of time are grouped together and viewed on the credit report as one incident, but be cautious of this too because some companies delay a credit report by a few days after your application. So, if you have been shopping around for ways to build your credit score and getting various inquiries they may and may not add up together over time.

Ranges
Excellent0-1
Good Credit 1-2
Fair Credit 3-4
Poor Credit 5-8
Bad Credit 9+

Extra about the credit score

A few more things to note about the credit score. Often times you will see that there are differences in your credit score among the credit reporting companies. It is worth noting that each of the reporting companies uses its own proprietary formula for calculating credit scores that are not available for public view (or scrutiny). This means that the way Equifax calculates your credit score will be different than how TransUnion does it. Another variable to consider is that creditors do not always report to every credit reporting company, which could alter a score for a particular reporting company. Often times, scores are fairly close, but if your scores have a wide range, you may want to research why (that means digging into your credit report for some answers!).

Chapter 13: Why Increase Your Credit

Limit

Before we look at how or when to increase your credit limit, we need to come up with a reason why you should do it, or why you should not to dit.. If you don't know some good reasons for why you should do this, you are unlikely to follow through with it. Here are some good reasons to request a credit limit increase:

- **It can help your credit score in the long run** – This is the biggest reason that you should look at increasing your credit limit. 30 percent of your credit score can be dependent on your credit utilization, or what percentage of your credit that you are using.

To use real numbers, let's say that you have a credit limit of $1,000, and you have a $500 balance on the card. Your credit utilization would be 500/1000, or 50%. This is a very high percentage, and would likely hurt your credit score. However, let's say you were able to increase that credit limit to $2,000, while keeping the same balance. Suddenly, your credit utilization would be cut in half – 500/2000 = 25%. A good rule of thumb is that you should aim to have a credit utilization rate of 10% or lower. Obviously, the higher your credit limit, the more achievable this will be.

In short, you want to owe as little money as possible relative to the amount of money that you could owe. There are two ways to do this… paying down debt is the best way, but that is not always feasible. Another way is to increase the amount of borrowing power you do have (though this does not mean that you should spend that extra amount, or else you will be even worse off, which should go without saying).

– **You have more credit in case of an emergency** – If you are responsible with your credit card and paying it off every month, a higher credit limit could provide you with peace of mind that if an emergency were to come, you would have more credit available to you. Ideally, of course, you would never have to use it, but it can be nice to know it's there.

If your limit is pretty low, the higher amount could be beneficial just for being able to make larger purposes. It all comes down to being responsible... if you are responsible and pay off your balance, it can be very helpful in many ways to have that extra money available. It could also be nice to have that higher limit if you are going on vacation, or doing home repairs, or anything that requires extra spending for a short time. The last thing you want to be worried about in these cases is running into your credit limit.

– **Increase your rewards** – Again, this is a good reason to get an increased limit only if you are responsible with your card and paying it off each month. Let's say you have a rewards credit card with a $1,000 limit. If you are going to be making a large purchase, you might not be able to fit it all on the card, thereby decreasing the amount of rewards you could get. An increased credit limit would help in this situation, because you could then maximize the rewards. This probably does not come up all that often, but it could, especially if you are making purchases for a business with the card.

If you are consistently running into your limit and have to use an alternate card, you may not be maxing out your rewards as much as you possibly could be.

– **If you NEED the extra money, that is NOT a good reason** – If you are looking at requesting an increase because you find yourself constantly in danger of going over the limit, this is NOT a good reason to try to increase it. This is a good reason to look at your spending. If you are desperate (and they will be able to see this), then they will likely turn you down.

Chapter 14: The Fair Credit Reporting Act

As a consumer, you have specific rights with regard to the information that the credit bureaus are sending out about your ability and past repayment history. You can remove negative information contained in your credit report using the rights given to you by the Fair Credit Reporting Act.

As you'll see in the following pages, much of the derogatory information that can enter your report can be challenged or even erased if you dispute the accuracy or correctness of the items. In addition, many of the negative items on your credit report must be deleted within a certain time limit.

The Fair Credit Reporting Act is a Federal Law passed by the United States Congress, which places certain restrictions and responsibilities on credit reporting agencies. This Federal Law gives consumers specific rights designed to assure maximum possible accuracy of items contained in their credit file. It attempts to ensure that credit reporting agencies (credit bureaus) exercise their responsibilities fairly.

Understanding Credit Reports and Credit Scores

Your credit report and credit score are the two primary methods that lenders and creditors make credit decisions about you.

When you apply for a credit card or loan, either your credit report or credit score (or both) are checked to see if you have a history of late payments on your accounts.

Mortgage lenders review your credit report for previous loan defaults. Credit reports are used to make a number of critical decisions that go far beyond your ability to obtain credit cards and loans. These include renting an apartment, obtaining insurance, and seeking employment. Even the utility company checks your credit report and credit score before turning on your electric service.

You will want to make sure that your credit reports are accurate and up to date.

Credit Report

Your credit history - loans, credit cards, collections, some medical bills, etc. - is compiled into a single document known as your credit report.

Just as your report card tracks your success in school, a credit report tracks your success in managing money responsibly. Right now, you may be more concerned about the grades on your report card, but your current financial habits can carry over and affect your ability to get credit as an adult.

A credit report is simply a record of your personal financial transactions, or credit history. It is a detailed summary of your bill paying history and the current status of your credit accounts. It documents who you owed, how much you owed, how much you paid, and, most importantly, how efficiently you paid those bills.

While each company's report may look different, they all have the same basic information indicating your credit activity:

The first section includes information used to identify you: your complete name, current address, previous address, social security number, date of birth, and your occupation, employer's name and address, and marital history.

Next, there is the credit history section. This includes information about credit that you have, such as your auto loans, mortgages, credit card accounts, and student loans. It may also include the terms of your credit, how much you owe your creditors, and your history of making payments. It will contain the names of creditors, the credit account number, the subscriber number, type or nature of each account, the dates of the accounts' opening, the credit limits of these accounts, outstanding balance, current status of each account, and your monthly payment schedule.

Your credit report also provides information about any bankruptcy you have filed, court judgments against you, or whether you have tax liens against your property.

Following this section is the details of inquiries about you. It shows institutions, companies or persons who recently reviewed your report. When you apply for credit, and sign the application form, you are authorizing the creditor to check your financial history.

There is a portion of the report that most people are not even aware. This portion is known as the "consumer statement." It allows you to provide explanations or make arguments up to one hundred words in length about items on the report with which you disagree.

Review your credit reports annually to make sure there are no mistakes — especially before you make a big purchase like a car or house, where you'll need to apply for a loan.

Credit Score

The information in your credit report can be given a numerical value called a credit score. The score summarizes your credit history and it helps lenders predict how likely it is that you will repay a loan and make payments when they are due.

While your personal financial transactions on your credit report detail your current and past borrowing history, a credit score is a number that reflects your creditworthiness.

When you apply for credit, lenders want to know what risk they take in lending you money. Your credit score gives them an idea of your creditworthiness at the moment in time when they check it. It has an impact on whether you can get new credit and the terms, including the interest rate, that lenders offer you. And your score changes over time as your financial situation changes.

The score ranges from about 300 to 850, with the higher score reflecting a lower risk for the lender. In general, a credit score of 680 or above is considered good.

The most popular credit score is the FICO score, named for Fair Isaac Corporation, the company credited with developing the score.

Lenders also use slightly different credit scores for different types of loans. If the information about you in the credit reports of the three major credit reporting agencies is different, your credit score from each of the agencies will be different.

How Are Credit Scores Calculated?

The more you know about how your credit score is calculated, the easier it becomes to improve your score and build good credit. A higher credit score means that your credit applications are more likely to be approved, and with more favorable interest rates.

Your credit score is calculated based on five factors, each carrying different weight in the overall equation.

Let's start by taking a look at how the computers calculate your score and how much weight is given to each category.

The percentages below are based on the five categories for the general population.

35% - Payment History

This is simply a record of whether you have paid your bills on time. As we all know, late payments are bad. Charge-offs, collections, bankruptcies, judgments, and foreclosures fall into this category.

30% - Amount Owed

This looks at your "utilization ratio" - how much you are using of the total credit you have available. Lenders believe that borrowers who are close to maxing out their credit are more likely to miss payments. Ideally, you want to have your balances at around 30%-35% of the limit.

15% - Length of Credit History

This is determined by the average age of your accounts, as well as how long it's been since those accounts were used. The longer you have had an account with a positive history, the more likely you will continue to pay your bills on time.

10% - Types of Credit

Most scoring models like to see a mix of different types of credit. Ideally, a mortgage loan, an installment account such as a student loan or car loan, and 4-5 revolving accounts such as credit cards. Lenders like to know that you can manage different kinds of accounts responsibly.

10% - Inquiries

This shows how often you have opened new accounts. Credit scoring models don't like to see a lot of inquiries for multiple types of accounts in a short amount of time. Opening a bunch at once will hurt your score. This usually indicates financial instability and someone is searching for money to get out of a bind.

Chapter 15: The Importance Of Credit

Score

If you don't have the cash or money to pay for something outright such as a car or a house, you will apply for credit, usually from the bank. This is akin to a loan that they give you which is to be returned with interest in the future. Of course, the bank does not simply give out loans to anybody. The bank needs to ensure that the person is to be trusted to return the money in the future, and to determine that, the bank usually checks the person's credit history.

A good credit score plays an extremely important role in your everyday life because it essentially acts as social proof that you are good with your finances and that you have a good track record of returning your loans on time. With a good score, you will have no difficulties with all the following:

1) **Personal Relationships**: Yes, relationships should not be started on the

basis of money. But it is hard to argue that it doesn't play a role in the success of a marriage or relationship. Research has shown that money is the number one reason why couples get a divorce in a marriage.

2) Buy a House: Buying a house is a very important decision because it is one of the best investments you can make for your future. You can bank on it to appreciate in value or rent out your room to make passive income. Unfortunately, a house is difficult to obtain if you have a poor credit history.

3) Find a Job: This one might be a little new to you but employers are now running credit checks on prospective employees. This is more commonly found in the government sectors where the hiring criteria is more stringent.

4) Getting a Good Loan: As of now, banks are still willing to give out to people with poor credit history because of their need for financial assistance. However, the process will not be as straightforward as if you have excellent credit history. Your loan interest rate is also likely to be much higher than usual. Keeping your credit score high will save you money on those high interest rate.

How are credit scores calculated?

There are 2 main types of scoring system out there:

1) FICO Score – The range of FICO score is 300-850. The average FICO score is about 689.

2) Vantage Score – The three credit agencies TransUnion, Experian and Equifax banded together to offer this alternative to FICO score. Although the same formula is used across the three credit agencies, the Vantage Score varies because the companies tap into different databases.

The concept of scoring is much more simple than how it sounds. The truth is – they all use a similar formula and the variances in the scores are mostly based on their databases containing differently reported information.

The credit score is derived from a mathematical formula that takes into account of all your credit data include your debt level, credit history, payment behavior, personal income and many other factors. Furthermore, all these factors are dependent upon each other which makes it difficult to predict how your score might turn out.

The importance of credit in today's world is extremely significant and choosing to ignore this can be very detrimental to your financial health. Hence, you have to be aware of how to keep your credit history in good shape.

Chapter 16: Reasons For Why You Need A Good Credit Score.

These days, society is increasingly dependent on credit scores when it comes to making a wide variety of different decisions about your future. As such, if your credit isn't as good as you might like, it will affect more than just your rates on a loan or if you are eligible for a credit card. Your credit is essentially a history that shows how strict you have been when it comes to reliably paying bills on time in the past which means a wide variety of different individuals are going to be curious about it as a way of determining how you are likely to act in the future.

Credit Score Chart	
EXCELLENT	751 - 850
GOOD	701 - 750
FAIR	651 - 700
BAD	350 - 650

Your credit score can vacillate from 350, indicating you are an extremely high-risk investment, to 850, which indicates anyone who loans you money is almost certain to get it back. Additionally, your credit rating is typically shown via a numerical rating from 1 (very bad) to 9 (very good). Currently only about five percent of Americans have a credit rating of 500 or lower while about fifteen percent have a score above 800 with the majority falling between the 700 and 800 range.

Living arrangements: First and foremost, your credit score affects your ability to get a mortgage and what you will pay monthly and overall. A poor credit rating can also prevent you from successfully getting a mortgage at all, or even prevent landlords from renting to you as well.

This is due to the fact that many landlords consider a lease a type of loan, after all, they are loaning you're a place to live in exchange for rent each month. If you have a low credit rating, and they do decide to rent to you, be prepared to pay extra for the privilege of having a roof over your head.

Car payments: The quality of your credit will also affect whether you will be approved for a loan for the car you are interested in purchasing as well as what your interest rate is going to be. In this case, bad credit can limit your options as fewer lenders will be willing to work with you and those that do are generally going to charge more to balance out the risk you represent. This typically translates into repayments for longer periods of time (72 months as opposed to 60 or less) and higher overall payments each month.

Job search: While the first two scenarios are to be expected, many people will be surprised to learn that a low credit score can affect your employment prospects as well. While employers can't check credit scores, they can check credit reports and many do so as a routine part of the hiring process. Depending on the job, if you have a history of poor financial responsibility an employer may be hesitant to offer you the position you have been dreaming about. Likewise, when it comes to promotions, many companies check credit reports to ensure their executives won't give the company a bad name.

Starting a business: Those who are grinding away at a 9-to-5 aren't the only ones who need to worry about their credit score, if you are self-employed a negative credit score can have even more serious implications. If you are looking to start a business with a small business loan, then you can bet lenders will check your credit score and, as most new businesses tend to fail, they will be very selective about who they lend their money to.

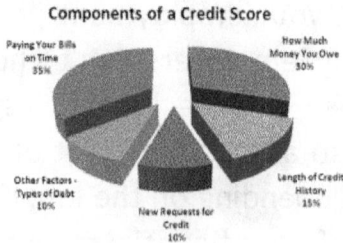

Components of a Credit Score

Monthly bills: Your credit score will also have an effect on many of your monthly bills including your utilities. Utility companies loan you their services every month and if your credit report shows that you are a risky investment then they will most definitely charge you more for the privilege of having electricity, running water, cellular service or cable and internet.

Techniques to rebuild credit.

Pay off what you owe: While this is going to be easier said than done in most situations, according to Experian, the ideal amount of credit utilization that you want is 30 percent or less. While there are other ways to increase your credit utilization rating, paying off what you owe on time each month will also go towards showing you can pay your bills on time, essentially pulling double duty when it comes to improving your credit score. It will also make it easier to follow through on the following tips.

Pay your credit card bills twice a month: If you have a credit card that you use on a regular basis, say for example because it offers you reward points, so much so that you max it out each month, it may actually be hurting your credit even though you pay it off in full at the end of each month.

This may be the case due to the way the credit card company reports to the credit bureau; depending on when they report each month it could show that your credit utilization rate is close to 100 percent depending on what your credit line currently is, thus hurting your credit score. As such, paying off your credit card in two smaller chunks throughout the month can actually help boost your credit without costing you anything extra overall.

Increase your credit limit: If you aren't currently in a position to pay down your credit card balance, you can still improve your credit utilization rate by increasing your current credit limit. This is an easy way to improve your credit utilization rate without putting any more money out up front. If you do this, however, it is important that you don't take advantage of the increased credit line as if you find yourself up against the limit again you will be worse off than when you started.

Only pursue this option if you have the willpower to avoid racking up extra charges, especially if you are already strapped when it comes to the payments you need to make each month; decreasing your credit utilization limit while also making more late payments is a lateral move at best.

Open a new account: Improving your credit utilization rate is one of the best ways to start rebuilding your credit. If your current credit card company won't increase your credit limit you may way to try applying for another credit card instead. If your credit is not so hot then your rates are going to be higher, but this won't matter as long as you don't plan on using the card in the first place.

Remember, credit utilization rate is a combination of your total available lines of credit so this can be a good way to drop your current utilization rate substantially, especially if you won't be able to pay off what you currently owe for a significant period of time.

Keep in mind, however, that if you choose this route then you are only going to want to apply for one new card every couple of months, especially if you aren't sure if you are going to be approved, as too many hard credit inquiries will only cause your credit score to drop, even if you do end up with a better credit utilization rate as a result. Spreading out these requests will give the inquiries time to drop off naturally and will prevent you from looking desperate to potential lenders which can also make it more difficult to get a new card.

Authorized users: If you don't have the credit to get a new credit card, or even to extend your current credit line, then your best choice may be to find someone you trust and ask them to become an authorized user on their card.

While most people will likely balk at the idea, you may be able to pacify them by explaining that you don't need a copy of their card or have any intent on using it, simply being listed on the card is enough to improve your credit utilization rating. Not only that, but you will also get credit for the on-time payments that this other person makes as well.

Chapter 17: Create A Personal Financial Blueprint

A financial blueprint serves as a plan for your financial growth and stability. Much like the blueprint for a house, this is the vision for the way your finances will look after a given period of time.

The blueprint is the framework of the larger plan. Spending, investing and saving all fall into this framework. The financial blueprint should be the first thing you consider and the basis for all major financial decisions.

The first step to creating a financial blueprint is to **establish clearly defined financial goals**. When we have defined and written out our goals, they become tangible. We can see them and take actionable steps to achieve them.

Example:

My goal is to save $2000 over the next twelve months.

Steps: Save $77.00 from each paycheck in a high interest savings account, until I've reached my goal.

On a bi-weekly pay schedule, with 26 pay periods in a year, I'd save $2002 over twelve months, not including the accumulated interest.

The next step to creating a financial blueprint is to **develop a budget**. A budget makes it easier to plot out just how much you will spend, save and/or invest. We will discuss how to create a budget in detail in the next chapter.

For many people retirement is a major concern. You can develop your financial blueprint to include retirement planning.

Your financial blueprint may also include college funds if you or your children plan to attend college and you want to mitigate student loan debt.

Investment plans, stocks and other savings methods can all go into the financial blueprint.

The financial blueprint is your personal plan to obtain financial freedom and is yours to create the way you wish.

Financial planners are there to help you work out your financial blueprint, however they come at a cost. If you are comfortable paying for advice on creating a financial plan then you might want to search out a planner in your price range, who will listen to your goals and consider your circumstances, and take your financial future seriously.

If a financial planner isn't for you, there are several FREE apps, and online tools to help build your financial blueprint. At the very least, they can help you get started on a budget and keep track of spending.

Chapter 18: Not Having A Plan To
Improve Your Credit

With the blink of an eye, your credit score can be change dramatically. Creditors are always reporting to the bureaus, and then you can toss in the threat of identity theft, and your credit score can come crashing down suddenly. So you need to create a plan for maintaining your credit score. Failing to create a plan is amongst the largest mistakes you could ever make.

☐ Create a Budget
☐ Be frugal if you're currently in debt
☐ Use technology to maintain and increase your credit score. ☐ Always review your monthly credit card bills and bank statements ☐ Pull your credit report every 6 months
☐ Always use the same name when applying for credit
☐ Keep you accounts active
☐ Protect your credit before, during and

after a divorce ☐ Work to raise your credit score to at least 720

Delaying Steps to Improve Your Credit

Most people don't consider credit important in their younger years. Most think, "I'm not ready to buy a house yet, so what's the big deal?" Just because you're not ready to buy a house doesn't mean you don't need good credit. Also remember, some employers are not hiring candidates with low credit scores. People with poor credit have higher interest rates on auto loans and credit cards. Even auto insurance premiums in some states are higher for individuals with low credit scores. Landlords are hesitating to approve applications from individuals with poor credit. So waiting to improve your credit is indefensible.

The deeper an individual's credit issues, the more likely a score can come back from the financial hardship that causes it and subsequent credit blemishes that occur when other situations arise.

It is also crucial that teenagers start establishing their credit while still living at home with their parents. This way when they leave home they are well positioned for the credit world that only recognizes them as a three digit number. This can be as simple as a joint credit card between the parents and the sibling, with control of the card in the hands of the parents.

Ignoring Your Credit All Together

There are many people out there with bankruptcies, foreclosures, repossessions, or other major delinquencies that just avoid credit entirely. The worst thing you can do for your credit is to wash your hands of it. Remember earlier when I said no credit is as bad as poor credit. Sooner or later you will need credit. By being a cash-only citizen, you will prolong the length of time that your score is too low to qualify for good interest rates, loans and credit terms.

If you have poor credit or no credit you can and should apply for credit immediately, even if you have had a bankruptcy. You can apply for a secured credit card; this is one that you have to put a deposit against, usually $300. It will mostly have a limit of $300, but if you use it wisely, your score will begin to climb. You should be shooting for the magical 720 credit score, which you may reach within 2-5 years if you follow these simple guidelines.

Chapter 19: What Is Credit And Why It's So Important To Fix Bad Credit Scores?

Most people already know and understand that credit makes up a big part of our everyday lives. That statement is so true because without credit. How can someone know whether you are good insurable assets?

Exactly, no one can tell whether you are a good person to lend money to and if they (bank, Mortgage Company, etc.) cannot tell, they will never take the risk on you. Therefore, you cannot purchase a car or get a mortgage which means you cannot buy that dream home of yours either. This is why credit is an important part of everyday lives. We all know that feeling; "you have been turned down, because your credit score is not quite what we can work with." Maybe we can get that loan, but the interest rate is so high that we are paying way too much for what we are purchasing.

Credit is all about money and assets. Remember you, me and everyone else use credit for many different reasons. It IS NOT just about buying a home or car; it can be used for many different things including larger purchases. However, good credit can allow you to take out a loan during a crisis you find yourself in and it can even protect you from frauds on occasions.

You can have a revolving credit and a fixed credit. With a revolving credit (Visa, MasterCard, Target credit card, or other retail store credit cards, you have a payment card or several but you repay the amount borrowed against items such as clothes and electronics, each month. With fixed repayment credit, this is where you repay things such as a mortgage or a car.

Why Should You Repay Your Credits?

To be honest, most people know all about credit or at least a general knowledge of it. However, many simply do not know much about how repaying credit really works. You could be one of them and it really can seem foreign to you.

Therefore, with a fixed repayment loan, you would make set repayments each month. You would pay back the amount you owe in installments maybe at the end of the month or week, depending on how the payment schedule has been set up.

Different loan amounts are paid back differently and over different periods of time, so let's say you had a mortgage, you would probably repay this over the course of say twenty years. If you choose less years, the payments would be more but if the repayments were to stretch over twenty years, the payments would be less.

However, this does not just work with mortgages; you can have a loan for almost anything. When you repay the loan back, you can then acquire another loan if you need it.

If you were however to choose a revolving credit option, you always have that credit. This could be anything from credit cards to charge cards but they work the same. You build up a certain amount of credit; you could charge items on a card and then repay the amount back each month.

However, you will always have access to this type of credit and to the credit that is not spent. Once you pay a part of the credit, you can reuse that credit again. So let us say that you have a credit of eight hundred dollars, and you used up five hundred dollars of credit, you only have three hundred left.

However, once you repay the money back, you have eight hundred dollars to spend again. These types of loans help to establish your credit and that is just one important reason why you need to keep repaying ANY and ALL loans, and of course your bills on time each month.

If you do not repay your loans back, your credit will be severely affected, lowers your credit score! Of course, you probably know this but it never hurts to have a reminder or two!

Why Is It Important To Have Good Credit And Fix Bad Credit Scores?

To be honest, you can in fact forget how important your credit score is. You can think everything is fine and that your credit is at a good place now, however, unless you are sure, it is a terrible attitude to take. What is more, you always seem to think that one little missed payment is not going to make a difference – it does!

One missed payment may not seem a lot of bother to anyone but that missed payment could be the difference in having an average credit score and a terrible one! However, even a past debt that you have not taken care of can still be bad for you – two years down the line. Your credit can suffer still.

So why is good credit that important? Well, when the time comes to go for a loan to purchase a new car or get a mortgage, you can find that were turned down for that loan. That is right; your credit is stopping you from being able to buy that dream home of yours or that big beautiful car! It is all down to your credit.

What is more, the only time when many people, including yourself, can stop and think about how important your actual credit is, is when you need a loan desperately and find you cannot get one. That is when you really will find yourself in a dangerous position because it could be an absolute emergency when you need to borrow money.

Most people do eventually borrow money in their lives and if your credit is not good, you might never be able to get another loan again. Those little emergencies kick you into touch as to how important your credit is because you really need the cash but you simply cannot get a loan anywhere.

For many, it is too late but it is never too late to change your credit. You can and should have good credit and it is vital for today and for your future. You might think your credit is OK now but you can never be sure and to be honest, if you have good credit, it means you could potentially be able to get a loan whenever you need it.

Of course, you might not be able to have perfect credit but having a good credit score at least can and is Very important. However, bad credit and bad credit scores can be changed and you can start changing it today!

Chapter 20: Pay By Your Report Date And

Not Your Due Date

We all have a habit of paying our dues right on the due date and never before. This is wrong especially if you want to increase your credit score faster than others. A secret which most people do not know is to start paying your bills by your report date and not your due date. This means, you need to start paying off your credit card before you reach the due date because this shows more reliability on your credit report.

☐Automate- the best way to stay away from late payments is to automate your payments. If you have an online banking account, get automate payment feature activated as soon as possible. Automatic bill payment is a fantastic way to make sure that you do not accidentally miss your payments because you lost your mail or you just misplaced it. Automate is a great way to show consistency in your payment history.

A lot of people have started using this feature because for instances where you need to leave town on an emergency, you may forget your bills and it would ultimately show as a late payment in your credit report. However, if you have automated all your payments, you do not have to worry about different dates and different payments because it would be taken care by your bank.

☐ Pay Twice A Month- if you are a person who goes close to your credit limit every month, even if you pay your balance in full, it can still affect your credit score. Your credit score can be drastically affected by how much you are charging versus your credit limit. So the best way is to pay off your bills in installments. You can pay one installment before the closing date and one after it. Your credit score can drop up to 40 points the moment you start closing to your credit limit.

Do not wait till your due date to pay off your bills because, chances are that other emergencies would pop up and you might have to share the budget. However, if you focus only on paying back your debts every time a little extra money pools up, you can achieve your target faster than you think.

Every consistent payment that you make towards your bills directly reflects in your credit score and your credit report. So if you want to boost your credit score, the best way is to start paying your dues on time and finish it off as soon as possible. The main goal here is to show consistency in payments in your credit score and portray you as a stable and reliable borrower.

Chapter 21: Important Credit Related

Terms You Need To Note

In this first chapter, I will explain to you some of the important terms that you need to understand before you go about learning the ways in which you can fix your bad credit.

These terms need to be understood thoroughly, so that you can evaluate your score card in a better way and understand as to what term stands for what.

Credit score

A credit score is a three digit number that is issued to a person depending on his/ her creditworthiness. The general range scale for this activity is between 300 and 850. It is like a report card that is issued to a person to tell them how worthy of credit they are and allow them to present it to lenders, banks, creditors etc. at the time of borrowing loans. It is also a score to tell others of how likely you are to pay your bills and how much you can be trusted in terms of paying any outstanding balances.

Credit report

A credit report is a report prepared for an individual or a firm to evaluate their financial transactions and understand their creditworthiness. It is used to check and record a person or firms credit borrowings, credit payments, late payments, no payments, bankruptcy etc. The credit report is what is used to create a credit score. To prepare the credit report, you are required to avail a credit form from your bank, store or Credit Card Company and duly fill it. It is then sent to a credit bureau; who check it and create a credit report and maintain a copy with themselves.

Creditworthiness

Creditworthiness of a person or firm states how much they can be trusted when it comes to issuing loans or lending money. It is no secret that these days, there are a lot of frauds out there and every type of creditor, be it banks or money lenders, prefer to first thoroughly go through a person's creditworthiness and only then issue credit. So it is important for a person or firm to have good creditworthiness, in order to maintain credit cards, avail loans, borrow money etc.

Good credit scores

Here are some scores for you to understand where you currently stand.

☐300-580: at this rate, you will either be denied a loan or credit or offered one at very high interest rates.

☐581-650: At this rate, you may avail a loan or credit but at a high interest rate.

☐651-710: At this rate, you will be given a loan or credit but at moderate interest rates.

☐711-750: At this rate, you will be given credit at a nominal interest rate.

☐751 and up: At this rate, you will get a loan or credit at the lowest possible interest rates available in the market.

Remember that the higher the score the better it is for you and the lower the score the worse your credit.

National credit agencies

When it comes to giving credit scores and evaluating your credit reports, you can get it done through 3 agencies. These three being Experian, Transunion and Equifax. These three will collect a fee for their service but they are sure to give you an accurate result. You can visit their websites and apply for the forms which need to be filled to help prepare your credit report and score. They can use a method best suited to create a credit score like the FICO system which was developed by Fair Isaac Corporation. There are also some sites out there who say they will do the scoring for free but you must check it before divulging your details.

Credit limit

Credit limit refers to how much a person or firm is allowed to borrow from a creditor on a given card or per account. This is important as it will allow the creditor to keep track and also not end up lending huge sums, which might not be repaid by the borrower. This limit is also beneficial for the borrower, as it will help him/ her plan better and also come up with a good plan to repay it on time without inviting any trouble. This limit is set after checking the person's creditworthiness and also going through their credit report.

Default

A default refers to failing to pay a certain sum of money back to the creditor or bank. It means that the person has failed to pay the money or the interest on the sum borrowed and not met a financial obligation. This generally happens when the debtor is unable to make the payment owing to not having enough finds or not being able to raise any or if he/ she are not willing to honor the debt and states that he/ she is not legally bound to make the payment. This practice can be extremely bad for the credit score.

Bankruptcy

Bankruptcy refers to a debtor announcing that he/ she is unable to pay for the borrowed sum and has no money left. Under such circumstances, the creditor intervenes to weigh the debtor's belongings and sells them off to raise enough money to pay off either the full or partial debt. This can also be sometimes filed on behalf of the debtor by the creditor themselves but it is a rare occurrence.

Bankruptcy code

Bankruptcy code is where the debtor is allowed to choose the type of bankruptcy that he/ she are going to file. This means that they can choose between liquidation- where a trusted third party sells their properties and pays the creditors, reorganization- where they are allowed to keep their properties and put it to good use to help earn money and pay creditors and a few other such arrangements.

These choices are not available to all and depend on their credit report. If they have a good report until bankruptcy was filed, then they can be granted reorganization and if they had a bad score then liquidation will be the only option left.

Chapter 22: What Matters And Can

Control

Most people don't know and don't care about, what the difference is between a Fico and a Vantage score is. And they shouldn't. We have no control over which score a lender uses nor will they usually tell us.

What we do care about finding out is how to manipulate the score to our best advantage. How do we make sure that our credit score is as high as possible? This is very important since our scores will affect:

The interest rate we will be charged

How much down payment is needed

Our insurance rates

Whether we can rent the apartment

Whether we get the job

And so much more

In order to manipulate anything, we must first know what it is, what it is comprised of, and how it works.

Let's start with "What is it"

A credit score is just a way of calculating your past experience, with credit, in order to have an educated prognostication as to how you will pay in the future. In other words "do you know how to handle credit and your budget?"

If you watch the TV commercials you would think that we all have 1 credit score. On TV the lady walks into the bank, throws her feet on the desk and announces that she "knows" that she has a wonderful credit score, thanks to the tools on XYZ company's website, and, therefore, demands "what can you do for me" from the loan officer. Is it really that simple? No.

My son recently went onto one of those websites that offer to give you your credit score for free and then went car shopping later that afternoon. On the free website, his score was 698 (very good) at the car lot his credit score was 655 (not so good). How can this be? Both scores were for the same person and on the same date.

I recently helped a friend with their home loan. Her credit scores were 723, 732 and 758, from the three major bureaus. That is a big discrepancy between scores.

How many credit scores do I have?

There are two things that affect how many scores we have, Reporting and Formulas.

The three major credit bureaus, Experian, Transunion and Equifax, each has a basic score for us. But these scores can vary significantly from each other. The scores are based on information sent to them by your creditors. The problem is that not all creditors report to all of the bureaus and they may also not report to each of them on the same date. For example, your credit card reports, to Experian, that your balance is $ 450 on August 1st but reports, to Transunion, that your balance is $ 535 on August 15th and does not report to Equifax at all. Two of the bureaus have correct information about your account, although different, and one bureau has nothing at all. This is a reporting issue and makes your score different for each bureau.

A home loan company, credit card, and a car dealer run your credit report, from the same bureau, at the same time of the same day. Each of these companies gets a completely different credit score for you. Why?

We have different scores because there are different scoring models set up for many different lenders and lending categories. Each model gives a different value to the information that is on your credit report. For example, the credit model that a car dealer would use will give more value to the information about how you paid on your last car loan than what is being reported by your favorite store card, the credit model set up for home loan companies would give more value to your past home loan payment history than to other accounts, etc.

There are probably hundreds of different scoring models, which means that each model may give you a different score on any given day. This is the formula issue.

Scores can vary from a low of 300 to a high of 850. So how is your score(s) calculated?

Chapter 23: Positive Steps To Boost Your

Score

When it comes to giving advice on boosting your credit score, most people will stop at having you analyze your credit report and disputing those errors. Beyond that, the advice is usually to pay your bills on time, and don't take out too much credit. However, if you really want to improve your credit score, you'll have to be more pro-active when it comes to managing it.

This starts with gaining more knowledge about what credit really is and what it means to have it. Educating yourself is key to learning how to better control moving forward.

Most people only understand credit from the back end. They know that their credit reports can reflect negatively or positively and could be the deciding factor on whether or not they're approved for that mortgage or automobile loan. But there is much more involved than that. The more you are aware of how credit works behind the scenes, the better able you'll be to steer your own in the right direction.

We all know that we have basic needs to sustain us. We need to have a home, sustenance, and clothing. Ideally, over the years you want to build up some sort of income to rely on you when you retire. To do this, you need to be able to earn enough money to take care of these basics and have a little left over to put away in a savings account.

When used properly, credit can be the means to your end goals. In a perfect world, you would like to see a situation where your money is put to use in an area that can help it to grow and begin to work for you. For the majority of us, working right up until the very last day of our life is not possible so when you know exactly how to use credit to help you do that, you're halfway to your goals.

Bottom line, you need to become more aware of how credit can affect your life.

Ask yourself the following questions, the answers will help you to get a better understanding the role credit should play and why you need it.

Why is credit important to me? In the simplest of understanding, credit is an arrangement where you can obtain something now and pay for it later. For most, it is important because it gives you immediate access to valuable resources when you don't have the money at the time. But the one fact most people fail to remember; it is the use of someone else's money that makes this happen. Without credit, it becomes increasingly difficult to meet a higher standard of living and maintain it.

What do I want to accomplish with credit? There are many reasons why one might choose to have credit. For some, it is a declaration of their trustworthiness. Others may want it as a show that they have reached a certain level of responsibility. When you enter into a credit agreement, you establish a relationship with another entity. How you use that credit will show if you have financial integrity or not. The possession of these qualities will allow you to use your credit in a way that can and will benefit you financially in the future. You can use it to acquire assets that you may not be able to get without it. It can be used to borrow money for things you need to help you lay the foundation for a particular lifestyle.

What is the difference between credit and debt? Most people get these two confused. Being in debt is the matter of owing money to another entity. Having credit means that you have made a promise to pay something back that you have borrowed. In most cases, that payback also includes paying a little extra in the form of interest. When you borrow something on credit, it means that the lender is confident that you not only have the **ability** to pay it back but also the **integrity** to pay it back.

By familiarizing yourself with what it really means to have credit, it can help you to resist the tendency to use your credit unwisely. You will stop to think before you choose to sign a contract or an agreement to get credit you don't need. Once you have grasped the finer points of credit, you should then turn your attention to your credit illness so you can begin to restore your good name.

Credit Habits

It may surprise you to hear that there are a lot of people that have very good credit habits but have low credit scores. It's hard to believe, but it happens more often than you might think.

There are a number of reasons why this might happen. You may pay your bills diligently for a time, but one day you may lose your job, end up in an accident, or have to deal with a major illness or other issues with you or someone in your family. When you don't fully grasp the purpose of credit, the common knee-jerk reaction is to use your credit to deal with the hard times.

This strategy may work for a little while, but as the bills begin to pile up, each month it will become more difficult than ever to keep your head above water. Before you realize it, your repayment plan begins to fail, and you're unable to keep up. The result is negative marks on your credit score.

The question then is how to create a plan that will allow you to maintain your credit health even during those hard times. Sometimes it is just a matter of focusing on **not** using your credit when you're not sure how to pay it back.

In general, credit is the easy fix that most people turn to when things get rough. However, if you seek out alternative options before you hit those rough patches, then you won't be faced with the need to repair your credit later. By doing this, you develop good credit habits that will carry you along even when times get hard.

When contemplating this, take the time to look back on what affected your credit score in the first place. You will usually recognize that it has something to do with poor credit habits. Perhaps you thought of using your credit cards for an expensive vacation, or you couldn't resist going on that shopping spree with your friends. Or maybe it was because something bad happened and you didn't have an alternative plan in place beforehand, and you went to your automatic relief button, your credit card. Whatever it is, in most cases, a poor credit score usually starts long before you make that first charge with how you view credit and how you handle it.

Take the time to analyze your behavior towards money and credit. What do you do every day? Do you have to have that gourmet coffee on your way to work every morning? Do you have an impulse to fill out a credit application for every place you go whether you need it or not? What are your shopping habits? Are you constantly in search of a new credit card to add to your collection?

Believe it or not, it takes just as much effort to build up a bad credit report as it does to build up a good one. The only difference is that those with a bad credit report don't think about their decisions as much. It all comes down to what your habits are.

Good credit habits include more than just paying bills on time. It also includes monitoring and managing your credit on a regular basis. It involves thinking before you sign or swipe and knowing how to prioritize your finances, so you are less likely to find yourself underwater. So, rather than looking at how much you can buy and pay for, try looking at whether or not the purchase is necessary and if it fits in with your financial goals for the future.

Take a close look at your daily, weekly, monthly, and yearly habits to see where you are weak when it comes to credit management. This weakness can be identified as a credit illness, and you will have to start making plans to break that habit. Remember, your credit score is never set permanently. It is constantly changing. Even with a low credit score, by starting to practice good credit management, your FICO score will see a very fast improvement, sometimes in just a matter of weeks.

This is not to say that you can't make a frivolous purchase every now and then. We all like to pamper ourselves, buy gifts for our friends, take vacations, or provide whatever objects of desire we might want. There is nothing inherently wrong with that. However, your primary focus is to sustain your lifestyle without harming your financial image. To do that, sometimes you may have to learn to say no to many of the desirable things you want.

Take the time to look back at your credit history over the past. Identify your credit illnesses (or bad habits) that have caused your score to drop. Remember, the definition of insanity is doing the same thing over and over again but expecting different results. There is a reason why your score is low, and you're reading this book. So, think about trying a new approach to rebuild your credit and get back on the right path. Once you do that, you are already on the path to credit recovery.

Creating a Plan

The way to devise a plan is to start with a clear picture of how much debt you actually have. You need to know just how much money you are paying bills every month. This list will become your primary source for payment. These are the bills that you will pay first before you make any additional purchases.

Once you have allocated and set aside money for the bills, you already have, turn your attention towards your regular spending habits. If you make a habit of writing down everything you buy and why, even the smallest item, you'll be amazed at how much money you're spending without even thinking about it. Do this for a week and then go back and review every detail. Mark off everything that you see as unnecessary and total that amount up.

The result could add up to a significant amount of money. Money that could be put to much better use if you had the self-discipline to control your spending habits.

Of course, we don't want to tell you to never spend on a little extra on something, but now that you know how much you're spending in that area, you can decide just how much money you want to commit to those extras.

Remember, your goal is to boost your credit score, so that means you'll have to spend something. We've already learned that closing your account or paying off a bill doesn't really have a heavy impact on your score, but spending and paying it off does. Try making small purchases each month and paying them off early. This will be a tremendous boost to your credit score. Think about using your credit card to make purchases, even if you have the cash on hand and then using the cash to pay your bill will automatically cause your score to increase. You could take this a step further by paying on your card twice a month instead of when the bill comes and see how fast your score will go up.

To be successful with these strategies, it is important that you make it a habit of documenting everything. It may seem like an extra chore, but when everything is recorded down on paper, it becomes more real than figures dancing around in your head. The physical paper actually adds another element to your credit consciousness that will serve as a constant reminder to not stray off of your plan, and it will help to build credibility with any businesses that have already extended credit to you.

What You Should Record

When you are working on revamping your habits you need to focus your attention on some very specific areas.

Always know when a payment is due and make sure to pay ahead of time.

Only use 30% of your credit limit. This will keep your credit utilization ratio at an optimum. In fact, try to keep your credit expenditures below that amount whenever possible.

Never max out your credit limit. Your creditors are constantly monitoring your spending habits and will take advantage of what they learn about you. Remember, the more you spend, the more interest you will have to pay. That only serves the company and does nothing to benefit your creditworthiness.

Use your credit card instead of cash for any purchases you make. As long as you have the money on hand to pay for it, you can be confident that you will be able to pay the bill off when it comes.

Try to pay your bill twice a month or even weekly if possible. Your creditors will see that you don't really need the credit but are only using it for convenience.

Don't Overthink It

When all is said and done, the bottom line is it is just a matter of keeping track of the numbers. You want to make sure that you have more money coming in than going out every month. However, with most people, spontaneous spending is their downfall. So, by keeping accurate records of how much money you are spending every month, you can have better control over where your money is going.

If keeping these records feels like drudgery to you, keep in mind that the more you are aware of what is happening with your money, the more conscientious you will be about it.

It's not rocket science, but it does require commitment and dedication to make sure that you don't fall by the wayside after a bit. But what about if you don't have the money to pay for all the debt you have accumulated. What are your options then?

Chapter 24: Start Working The System

In this chapter, we will look at ways to proactively work the system so that you can improve your credit rating even further. There is a big disclaimer for this section, though – I am going to advise applying for credit – if you do not have the self-discipline to stop spending money unnecessarily (no judgement here, I used to spend money to make myself feel better) it is better to pay all your debt down and only keep one emergency card.

You Need Some Credit

I mentioned briefly that I had been where you are now – I too once had bad credit. That quite frankly is an understatement. At one stage, I excelled at living beyond my means. I would use one credit card to pay the next and was eventually in so much debt that I ended up having to move back home with my parents and having to sell my apartment at a loss to prevent foreclosure. I also had my car repossessed.

So, as you can see, my credit was destroyed!

As a result, when I started coming out from under it, I never wanted to see another credit card in my life again. I swore that if I couldn't afford to pay for anything cash, I would just go without it. This did work for some time but it did not help me to improve my credit score.

You see, although I had paid up all the arrears and gotten the negative listings removed, I was still considered a bad credit risk simply because I had no credit accounts at all. Now, how's that for irony – at first, I couldn't get credit because I had too much credit and then I couldn't get credit because I had no credit.

The problem with having no credit at all is that there is nothing that shows how well you can actually manage your debt. That is where the payment history comes back into play. When you have an active credit account and are paying it on time every month, you actually help to flesh out the picture of you as a responsible borrower.

Keep about two credit accounts so that you can show that you can manage your credit. You do need to keep them active, so do use them and make sure that they have a small balance on them. Do not max them out and pay them on time every month and your credit score will continue to rise.

Getting a Secured Credit Card

Of course, if you have no credit facilities because you were in a situation like mine, getting new facilities can be tough. What you can do is apply for a secured credit card. With a secured card, you will need to have money in some sort of savings account that can be offered as collateral against your spend on the card.

Your credit limit will match the funds that you have saved and you won't be allowed to exceed this but this can be a really great way to help to establish a credit history.

It is important to ensure that the card is actually a credit card and that you are not simply using the money in the savings so that you can ensure that you build your credit history.

Again, the normal rules apply – do not max out the card, always pay more than the minimum installment and make sure that the payments go through on time each and every month.

After you have established a good payment history – usually after about six months or so, enquire about switching to an unsecured credit card. Whilst a secured card does help to establish some payment history, it is not a true reflection of how you would handle a "real" credit limit and the information on the credit bureau would reflect that.

Get Installment Finance

Just like getting the credit card, having one installment credit facility on your profile helps to improve your overall credit rating and shows creditors that you are able to handle more than one type of finance.

Here again, though, you do need to let common sense prevail. If you have an existing loan, you do not need a second one. And do look for favorable rates and a good reason to get the money. "Improving my credit rating" is not a good excuse to borrow $20 000, for example. A small loan is all that is needed here so don't go applying for money for that overseas trip, etc.

The big advantage here is that the rates tend to be better because there is a set installment and you know that your debt will decrease each month. Not being able to draw down on the loan is one of the biggest benefits of installment finance versus credit card finance – at least you know that you will pay it off eventually.

Again, if you concerned that you will not be able to handle the payments, it is better to skip this step altogether.

Limit Credit Applications

Overall, it is best to limit the number of credit applications that you make. It is better to shop around for a good rate and apply at only one service provider than to apply at several. The reason for this is that every time you apply for a loan, an enquiry is made on your credit profile and potential creditors can view these enquiries as well.

Your credit score also does a bit of a hit when there are multiple enquiries over a short period of time. Think about for a second – if your friend was applying for money all over the place, would you think that they were desperate or would you think that they were credit worthy?

Don't apply for credit cards, store cards or loans unless you really need to and you can minimize the impact on your credit rating.

Be Consistent and Persevere

I wish I could tell you that if you did all these steps for a week, your credit rating would magically improve. Unfortunately, the system is not designed to work that way. Whilst there are things that you can do to improve your score, your past behavior will always play a role in your current credit score.

If you follow the tips in this book, you can expect to start seeing improvements in around about three to six months and the effects are cumulative as long as you are consistent in your efforts. Even if there is the odd setback, the cumulative efforts will soon start to bear fruit.

And just remember, the last six months are always given the most importance when it comes to determining your FICO score. Those looking over your credit report will also be more willing to give you a bit of leeway if they can see that you have made a real determined effort to improve the management of your financial affairs.

The benefits of being financially responsible are really worth the work – not only will you be able to save money on interest and insurance premiums but you might be in better standing to get the job of your dreams as well. And, best of all, you will have some peace of mind as well.

The Last Step

You will need to monitor your credit report to ensure that everything is on track. Take advantage of the free annual credit report to do a bit of a financial audit as well if your rating has improved. Call your insurance broker and have your policy reviewed. Do the same with your credit accounts as well – you might just manage to save some money on interest payments.

Make the steps that I have described in this book a habit – make it a priority to always pay your bills on time, never max out your cards, always pay a bit more than you have to and you will soon find that are once again in full control of your finances.

Chapter 25: Make Your Credit Age Older

Considering that older credit accounts are viewed more favorably by credit scoring agencies when it comes to determining your credit score, it follows that making your average credit age will help you achieve a higher credit score! And by increasing your average credit age, I don't mean waiting for the passage of time! I'm talking about a practical but relatively controversial method wherein you report a lost credit card.

How on earth can reporting a lost credit card make your average credit age older? It works this way. If you report a lost credit card, your credit card company will most probably close that account. But in terms of computing your average credit age, it's highly possible that credit-scoring agencies to which they report may still factor that closed account. In lieu of the closed account, your credit card company may open a new account for you, to which all of the closed account's history and data will be transferred. And guess what? It's highly likely that this new account will be considered by credit scoring agencies when they compute for your subsequent credit scores, thereby increasing your credit history's average age!

Essentially, reporting a lost credit card may have the effect of doubling that credit card's age. And that increase in age may increase your total average credit age, which can only be beneficial for your credit score! But keep in mind that this may not work with all credit scoring agencies. It's possible that some of them will treat this differently and may backfire on you. If you plan to use this tactic, proceed very carefully by making sure that your specific credit-scoring agency treats reported lost credit cards this way.

Conclusion

We have come to the end of the book. Thank you for reading and congratulations for reading until the end.

You now have an idea on how to repair your credit and repair it quickly. You do not have to delegate your repair strategies to a 3rd party that will charge you for their services. If anything, you are better off saving your money and seeking to know your financial situation intimately, and then troubleshooting the problems you find. Your best solution will be to mix short-term strategies with longer-term ones. This way, your progress will not slide at any point in the future.

Thank you and good luck!

www.ingramcontent.com/pod-product-compliance
Lightning Source LLC
Chambersburg PA
CBHW071226210326
41597CB00016B/1958